St. Thomas' Parish Registers

[Baltimore County, Maryland]

1732–1850

COMPILED BY

Bill AND *Martha Reamy*

HERITAGE BOOKS
2014

HERITAGE BOOKS

AN IMPRINT OF HERITAGE BOOKS, INC.

Books, CDs, and more—Worldwide

For our listing of thousands of titles see our website
at
www.HeritageBooks.com

Published 2014 by
HERITAGE BOOKS, INC.
Publishing Division
5810 Ruatan St.
Berwyn Heights, MD 20740

International Standard Book Numbers
Paperbound: 978-1-58549-105-6
Clothbound: 978-0-7884-9049-1

TABLE OF CONTENTS

ST. THOMAS' PARISH

INTRODUCTION

Some miles northwest of Baltimore City, on a shady hill overlooking Reisterstown Road, stands the parish church of St. Thomas, Garrison Forest. The parish was created by an Act of the Assembly at the session of 21 September-29 October 1742. The Act stated that St. Paul's Church in Baltimore County was located too far for the inhabitants of the Forest to attend regularly, and hence a new parish was to be created.[1]

Not wishing to lessen the income of the incumbent rector of St. Paul's, the Rev. Benedict Bourdillon, the legislators stipulated that the new parish was not to be created out of St. Paul's Parish until the "Death or Translation" of Bourdillon. The new parish was to embrace Soldier's Delight and Back River Upper Hundreds.[2]

Nelson Waite Rightmyer, in his Parishes of the Diocese of Maryland, published in 1960, states that after its creation, St. Thomas' Parish itself had several newer parishes taken from its jurisdiction: Western Run Parish (1844), Sherwood Parish (1859), Reisterstown Parish (1871), and Emmanuel Parish (1876), were all taken from the territory originally set aside in 1742 as St. Thomas' Parish. Thanks to an excellent series of maps prepared for Rightmyer's book, we can locate the boundaries of St. Thomas' Parish: Starting at York Road in Towson, running along Joppa and Old Court Roads to Liberty Road, northwest on that road to Deer Creek Road, north on that road to the line between Baltimore and Carroll Counties, and thence in a northeasterly direction to

Black Rock Road, southeast on that road, across Falls Road to a farm formerly belonging to Dr. Griffith, north to Hereford Road, east to York Road, southeast along what eventually becomes Corbett Road, southwesterly to the course of Loch Raven Reservoir to Cub Hill Road, southwesterly with Old Harford Road to the Joppa Road, and then along Joppa Road westerly to Towson and from there along Joppa Road to Old Court Road.[3]

The history of the parish and the activities of the rectors and parishes have been discussed in Ethan Allen's The Garrison Church,[4] and in Volume One of The Green Spring Valley Its History and Heritage, By Dawn F. Thomas.[5] For that reason this introduction will merely list the rectors who served the parish from its creation down to about 1825, when the volume of parish register entries ends.

The first rector, Rev. Thomas Cradock, a graduate of Magdalen College, Oxford University in England, served from 1745 until his death in May 1770. He was followed by Rev. William Edmiston, whose ministry was short: from 1770 to 1775. Reverend Thomas Hopkinson served from 1775 to 1776. Rev. John Andrews served St. Thomas' and St. James' Parishes from 1782 to 1785. Later rectors included Rev. Thomas Fitch Oliver (served 1793 to 1797), Rev. John Coleman (1799 to 1804), Rev. John Armstrong (1804 to 1810), Rev. John Chandler (1813 to February 1814), Rev. Joseph Jackson (1818 to 1819) and Rev. Charles Austin (1820 to 1849).[6]

This volume of births, deaths, and marriages, is taken from the microfilm of both the original and transcription of the register, at the Maryland Historical Society. Entries have been copied in the order of their appearance in the original register. Page numbers have not been entered because the photostat has two or more sets of page numbers, but the photottstat copy at the Maryland Historical Society does have its own index. To enhance the usefulness of the work, the compiler has included a number of supplementary sources: tombstone inscriptions published in Scharf's History of Baltimore City and County, and in Ridgely's [7] Historic Graves. Also included are lists of contributors to the building of the church, and a list of vestrymen and wardens, both taken from Allen's The Garrison Church. [8] Abstracts from the vestry proceedings (which were copied by Lucy H. Harrison) have been added, to give an insight into some of the activities of parishioners. Finally a copy of the "1763 Tax List of St. Thomas' Parish" with the names of the taxables arranged alphabetically by hundreds, has been included.

Some of the entries of St. Thomas' Parish have been published by the writer of this introduction. Taken from the copy of the register made by Lucy H. Harrison, marriages were published in the Bulletin of the Maryland Genealogical Society, and later were included in Maryland Marriages, 1634-1777, and Maryland Marriages 1778-1800. [9] Some of the births were abstracted from Miss Harrison's copy of the Register and published in the Maryland and Delaware Genealogist. [10]

Robert Barnes
August 1987

REFERENCES

1

Archives of Maryland:XLII:Proceedings and Acts of the General Assembly of Maryland (20) 1740-1744. Bernard Christian Steiner, ed. Baltimore: Maryland Historical Society, 1923, p. 418.

2

Ibid., pp. 420-421.

3

Nelson Waite Rightmyer. Parishes of the Diocese of Maryland. Reisterstown: Educational Research Association, 1960, p. 37

4

Ethan Allen. The Garrison Church. New York: James Pott and Co., 1898.

5

The Green Spring Valley: Its History and Heritage. (2 vols.). Volume One by Dawn F. Thomas. Baltimore: The Maryland Historical Society, 1978.

6

Ibid., pp. 143-154.

7

J. Thomas Scharf. History of Baltimore City and County. 2 vols. (1881). Repr., Baltimore: Regional Publishing Company, 1971. Helen W. Ridgely. Historic Graves of Maryland and the District of Columbia. Repr., Baltimore: Genealogical Publishing Company, 1967.

8

Allen, op. cit.

9

Robert Barnes, "Marriages in St. Thomas P. E. parish, Baltimore County, Maryland, 1729-1824." Bulletin of the Maryland Genealogical Society. Vol. 11 (1970), pp. 20-21, 70. Robert W. Barnes. Maryland Marriages, 1634-1777. Baltimore: Genealogical Publishing Company, 1975. Robert W. Barnes. Maryland Marriages, 1778-1800. Baltimore: Genealogical Publishing Company, 1979.

10

Robert W. Barnes. "Births Recorded in St. Thomas' Parish, Baltimore County, Maryland." Published serially in Maryland and Delaware Genealogist, beginning 24 (Winter 1983), 4-5.

BIRTHS

Christopher OWINGS, son of Samuel OWINGS and Urath his wife born the 16th day of February 1744.

Edward HAMILTON, son of John HAMILTON and Sydney his wife, born 20th November 1744.

Elizabeth MURPHEY daughter of William MURPHEY and Priscilla his wife, born the 25th September 1743.

Abigal HEMPY daughter of Frances HEMPY born the 12 June 1744.

Mary PRICE daughter of Phillip PRICE and Hannah his wife born 12 September 1743.
Phillip PRICE son of Phillip PRICE and Hannah his wife born 18th January, 1744.

Sarah HAYS daughter of Thomas HAYS and Ann his wife born 2d of March 1744.

Garret MALSTER son of Sarah MALSTER born the 28th day of October 1744.

Zechariah RISTON son of Edward RISTON and Rachel his wife born December 10th 1744.

Joshua BOND son of John BOND and Ceturah his wife, born 3 December 1740.
Ruth BOND daughter to the aforesaid John and Ceturah born 25th February 1744.

Elenor THOMAS daughter to John THOMAS and Sarah his wife born October 8th 1742.
Sarah THOMAS daughter of John THOMAS and Sarah his wife born 23rd March 1744.

Mary OURSLER daughter of Edward OURSLER and Ruth his wife, born the 9th of May 1738.
Elizabeth OURSLER daughter of the aforesaid Edward and Ruth born 28th October 1739.
Eli OURSLER son of the aforesaid Edward and Ruth born 8th October 1741.
Margaret OURSLER daughter of the aforesaid Edward and Ruth born 24th November 1743.

Rachel HAMMOND daughter of Lawrence HAMMOND and Abrarilla his wife, born July 31st 1733.
Mary HAMMOND daughter of the aforsaid Lawrence and Abrarilla born 22d April 1735.

BIRTHS

Thomas HAMMOND son of the aforesaid Lawrence and Abrarilla born
12th March 1737.
William HAMMOND son of the aforesaid Lawrence and Abrarilla born
25th December 1739.
Elizabeth HAMMOND daughter of the aforesaid Lawrence and
Abrarilla born the 12th March 1741.
Katharine HAMMOND daughter of the said Lawrence and Abrarilla
born 16th February 1744.

Peter BOND, son of Peter BOND and Susanna his wife born 14th day
April 1744.

Sarah WATSON daughter of William WATSON and Elizabeth his wife
born 8th January 1742.
Elizabeth WATSON daughter of the aforesaid William and Elizabeth
born 18th September 1744.

Patience KELLY daughter of James KELLY and Prudence his wife born
June 7th 1738.
Nathan KELLY son of James KELLY and Prudence his wife born 4th
July 1740.
Honnor KELLY daughter of James KELLY and Prudence his wife born
18th December 1742.
James KELLY son of James KELLY and Prudence his wife born 11th
February 1744.

Charles MASON son of Edward MASON and Sarah his wife, born 10th
day December 1743.
Richard BOND son of Richard BOND and Mary his wife, born 9th
September 1745.

Absalom ROBINSON son of John ROBINSON and Elizabeth his wife born
6th September 1745.

Thomas RANDALL son of Christopher RANDALL and Katharine his wife,
born January the 11th, 1726.
Bale RANDALL born 1 August 1728, died 20th October following.
Christopher RANDALL son of the aforesaid Christopher and
Katharine born September 25th, 1729.
William RANDALL son of the aforesaid Christopher and Katharine
born August 18th, 1731.
Rebekah RANDALL daughter of the aforesaid Christopher and
Katharine born 27th December 1733.
Hannah RANDALL daughter of the aforesaid Christopher and
Katharine born 27th October 1736.
Rebekah RANDALL daughter of the aforesaid Christopher and
Katharine born 5th December 1738.
Nicholas RANDALL son of the aforesaid Christopher and Katharine
born 27th February 1740.
Susanna RANDALL daughter of the aforesaid Christopher and
Katharine born 7th May 1743.
Bale RANDALL son of the aforesaid Christopher and Katharine born
17th August 1745.
George HOWARD son of Cornelius HOWARD and Ruth his wife, born
12th March 1740.

Rachel HOWARD daughter of Cornelius HOWARD and Ruth his wife
born 5th May 1743.

Joshua HOWARD son of Cornelius HOWARD and Ruth his wife born
September 29th 1745.

Thomas BAILEY son of George BAILEY and Mary his wife, born October
the 18th 1744.

John Cockey OWINGS son of Joshua OWINGS and Mary his wife, born
the 11th of January 1736.

Richard OWINGS son of the aforesaid Joshua and Mary, born the
13th November 1738.

Joshua OWINGS son of the said Joshua and Mary born the 22nd of
March 1740.

Edward OWINGS son of the said Joshua and Mary born the 1 day of
November 1743.

Michael OWINGS daughter of the said Joshua and Mary born the 12th
February 1745.

Thomas FORD son of John FORD and Ruth his wife, born the 20th
February 1744.

Edmund HOWARD son of Edmund HOWARD and Ruth his wife, born 11
September 1745.

Caturah RISTON daughter of Edward RISTON and Rachel his wife born
10th October 1745.

Richard GIST son of Thomas GIST and Susanna his wife, born 1
November 1745.

Harman BOND son of Peter BOND and Sushannah his wife born July
the 14th 1746.

John BARDELL son of Joseph BARDELL and Jane his wife, born August
12th, 1745.

Richard OWINGS son of Samuel OWINGS and Urath his wife born the
26 of August 1746.

Ruth HAMILTON daughter of John HAMILTON and Sydney his wife born
September 18th 1746.

Sarah OWINGS daughter of Richard OWINGS and Ann his wife, born
the 29th day of July 1738.

Rachel OWINGS daughter of the aforesaid Richard and Ann born 12
day of March 1741.

Richard OWINGS son of the aforesaid Richard and Ann born 20 March
1743.

Edward Stonestreet OWINGS son of the said Richard and Ann born
the 15th May 1746.

Joseph BARDELL son of Joseph BARDELL and Jane his wife born
January the 7th 1746.

BIRTHS

John METCALF son of John METCALF and Mary his wife, born the 27 February 1743.

William METCALF son of the above John and Mary, born the 6th January 1745.

James METCALF son of the said John and Mary born the 19th November 1746.

William HAMMOND son of Lawrence HAMMOND and Abrilla his wife, born 1st August 1746.

Henry DUNN son of Arthur DUNN and Margret his wife, born 20th March 1746.

John NORRIS son of Thomas NORRIS and Abririlla his wife, born 6th May 1746.

Mary NORRIS daughter of the aforesaid Thomas and Abririlla[sic] born February 6th, 1743.

Ruth HOWARD daughter of Cornelius HOWARD and Ruth his wife born 15th September 1747.

Elenor BOND daughter of Richard BOND and Mary his wife born February 15, 1732.

Ruth BOND daughter of the abovesaid Richard BOND and Mary his wife born December 5th 1734.

Mary BOND daughter of the above Richard and Mary born 25th December 1736.

Ann BOND daughter of aforesaid Richard and Mary born April 3d 1739.

Jemima BOND daughter of aforesaid Richard and Mary born 23d April 1741.

Nicodemus BOND son of the sd. Richard and Mary born 25th July 1743.

Elizabeth BOND daughter of aforesaid Richard and Mary born 30th August 1747.

George ASHMAN son of George ASHMAN and Jemima born 20th May 1740.

Josephus ASHMAN son of the abovesaid George and Jemima born 8th May 1745.

Nancy ASHMAN daughter of the said George and Jemima born 29th November 1747.

George SEABROOK son of William SEABROOK and Jemima his wife born 25th February 1747.

Floria LEMMON daughter of Johanna LEMMON born 15th May 1733.

Sarah JONES daughter of Richard JONES and Johanna his wife, born 18th October 1737.

Richard JONES son of Richard JONES and Johanna his wife born 24th May 1739.

Ann JONES daughter of Richard JONES and Johanna his wife born 9th July 1741.

4

BIRTHS

Joshua HURD son of John HURD and Ruth his wife born 22d of June 1740.

Sarah HURD daughter of John HURD and Ruth his wife, born 11th June 1742.

Priscilla MURPHEY daughter of William MURPHEY and Priscilla his wife, born 5th June 1746.

William MURPHEY son of William MURPHEY and Priscilla his wife, born 28th April 1748.

Caroline MASON daughter of Edward MASON and Sarah his wife born July 25th 1746.

Edward BOND son of Peter BOND and Susanna his wife, born 12th July 1748.

Nancy JACKS daughter of Richard JACKS and Ann his wife born 15th October 1747.

Elizabeth GIST daughter of Thomas GIST and Susannah his wife born 14 December 1736.

John GIST son of the aforesaid Thomas and Susannah born November 22d 1738.

Thomas GIST son of the aforesaid Thomas and Susannah born March 30th 1741.

Mordica GIST son of the aforesaid Thomas and Susannah born February 22d 1742.

Joshua GIST son of the aforesaid Thomas and Susannah born October 16th 1747.

Hellen HAMILTON daughter of John HAMILTON and Sydney his wife born 24 October 1748.

Butlar OWINGS son of Richard OWINGS and Ann his wife born the 24th of August 1748.

Richard Gott OWINGS son of Stephen OWINGS and Sarah his wife born January 18th 1744.

Capell OWINGS son of the aforesaid Stephen and Sarah born December 23rd 1746.

Samuel OWINGS son of the aforesaid Stephen and Sarah born 12 September 1748.

Priscilla HAWKINS daughter of John HAWKINS and Mary his wife was born 2d January 1733.

John HAWKINS son of the aforesaid John and Mary was born 14th February 1736.

Elizabeth HAWKINS daughter of the aforesaid John and Mary was born 1 June 1738.

Joseph HAWKINS son of the aforesaid John and Mary was born 11 January 1739.

Moses HAWKINS son of the aforesaid John and Mary was born 10th October 1742.

Rezin HAWKINS son of the aforesaid John and Mary was born 21 November 1743.

Ruth HAWKINS daughter of the aforesaid John and Mary was born 6 June 1746.

Thomas HAWKINS son of the aforesaid John and Mary was born 8 June 1748.

Elizabeth RICKETTS daughter of Thomas RICKETTS and Mary his wife was born the 30th day of November 1744.

Ruth RICKETTS daughter of Thomas and Mary his wife aforesaid was born the 4th June 1746.

Temperance ROBINSON daughter of John ROBINSON and Elizabeth his wife was born the 4th day of November 1747.

Edward MASON son of Edward MASON and Sarah his wife was born the 1st day of December 1748.

Joseph GIST son of William GIST and Violletta his wife was born the 30th day of September 1738.

William GIST son of the aforesaid William GIST and Violetta his wife was born 23rd September 1743.

Ann GIST daughter of the aforesaid William GIST and Violetta his wife was born the 16th day of September 1745.

Sarah GIST daughter of the aforesaid William GIST and Violetta his wife was born the 25th day of November 1747.

Vscilla WHIPS daughter of John WHIPS and Sarah his wife was born 9 April 1746.

Rachel WHIPS daughter of the aforesaid John WHIPS and Sarah his wife was born June 25th 1747.

Ruth WHIPS daughter of the aforesaid John WHIPS and Sarah his wife born February 13th 1748.

Rossanah SHIPLEY daughter of George SHIPLEY and Katharine his wife born 2nd February 1748.

Elizabeth PORTER daughter of Thomas PORTER and Elener his wife born 14th June 1747.

Ann CROSS daughter of Robert CROSS and Jemima his wife was born 27th November 1748.

John BUCKINGHAM son of Benjamin BUCKINGHAM and Abrilla his wife born the 6th March 1748.

Ann GORSNELL daughter of William GORSNELL and Sarah his wife born 8 February 1748.

Marcilla OWINGS daughter of Joshua OWINGS and Mary his wife was born the 5th July 1748.

Rachie ROBINSON daughter of John ROBINSON and Mary his wife was born January the 11th day 1747.

Larkin DORSEY son of Francis DORSEY and Elizabeth his wife born 15th February 1747.

Belinda FORD daughter of John FORD and Ruhamak his wife was born the 4th day November 1748.

Mary RICKETTS daughter of Thomas RICKETTS and Mary his wife was born the 4th day of July 1749.

Arthur CRADOCK son of the Rev. Thomas CRADOCK and Katherine his wife was born the 19th day July 1747.

Cloe KILLEY daughter of William KILLEY and Elizabeth his wife was born the 1(?)st day of August 1741.
Urath KILLEY daughter of William KILLEY and Elizabeth his wife was born the 9th day of February 1743.
Rachel KILLEY daughter of the aforesaid William KILLEY and Elizabeth his wife was born 19th February 1747.

Kathrine WINCHESTER daughter of William WINCHESTER and Lydia his wife was born 2d day of Novembver 1748.

John BOND son of Richard BOND and Mary his wife was born the 9th October 1749.

Rachel HOWARD daughter of Cornelius HOWARD and Ruth his wife was born the 14th day of October 1749.

Elizabeth SEABROOK daughter of William SEABROOK and Ziporah his wife was born the 29th day of December 1749.

Elizabeth HAILE daughter of Nicholas HAILE and Ruth his wife was born the 26th January 1746.

Nicholas BUTLER son of Aman BUTLER and Elizabeth his wife was born the 11th of August 1748.

Roger ROBINSON son of John ROBINSON and Mary his wife was born June the 3rd day 1750.

Elener BOND daughter of John BOND and Keturah his wife was born 22d October 1746.
Mary BOND daughter of the aforesaid John BOND and Keturah his wife was born the 25th June 1749.

Samuel OWINGS son of Richard OWINGS and Rachel his wife was born the first day of April 1702.

Urath RANDALL daughter of Thomas RANDALL and Hanah his wife was born the first day of January 1713.

Bale OWINGS son of Samuel OWINGS and Urath his wife was born the 9th day of May 1731.
Samuel OWINGS son of the abovesaid Samuel OWINGS and Urath his wife was born the 17th day of August 1733.

Rachel OWINGS daughter of the aforesaid Samuel OWINGS and Urath his wife was born the 2d day of May 1736.

Urath OWINGS daughter of the abovesaid Samuel OWINGS and Urath his wife was born the 26 June 1738.

Thomas OWINGS son of the abovesaid Samuel OWINGS and Urath his wife was born the 18th of October 1740.

Hanah OWINGS daughter of the abovesaid Samuel OWINGS and Urath his wife was born the 17th April 1743.

Richard OWINGS son of the abovesaid Samuel OWINGS and Urath his wife was born the 16th July 1749.

Elizabeth PINDELL daughter of John PINDELL and Elener his wife was born the 19th day January 1749.

Larkin RANDALL son of Christopher RANDALL and Katherine his wife was born the 10th June 1749.

Stevenson PLOWMAN son of Jonathan PLOWMAN and Eliza. his wife was born 24th June 1749.

John GILL son of Stephen GILL and Elizabeth his wife was born 2nd October 1709.

Mary GILL [sic] daughter of Nicholas ROGERS and Elener his wife born 1712.

Elizabeth GILL daughter of John GILL and Mary his wife was born 4th March 1731.

Elener GILL daughter of John GILL and Mary his wife was born 4th January 1735.

John GILL son of John GILL and Mary his wife was born 4th day of February 1737.

William GILL son of the aforesaid John GILL and Mary his wife was born 12th May 1739.

Stephen GILL son of aforesaid John GILL and Mary was born 1st day of January 1741.

Edward GILL son of the foresaid John GILL and Mary was born 2nd day of July 1744.

Sarah Gill daughter of the aforesaid John GILL and Mary was born 2nd January 1747.

John CRADOCK son of Thomas CRADOCK and Katharine his wife was born 25th January 1749.

Ruth GILL daughter of Stephen GILL and Urath his wife was born the 26th February 1745.

Mary GILL daughter of the aforesaid Stephen GILL and Urath his wife born 9th July 1747.

Stephen GILL son of the aforesaid Stephen GILL and Urath was born 7 February 1748.

Nicholas GILL son of John GILL and Mary his wife was born May the 25th 1750.

Hanah OWINGS daughter of Samuel OWINGS and Urath his wife was born the 27th January 1750.

William HAWKINS son of John HAWKINS and Mary his wife was born the 5th day of October 1750.

Ann BEASEMAN daughter of William BEASEMAN and Ruth his wife born 27th July 1740.

Joseph BEASMAN son of the aforesaid William BEASMAN and Ruth was born 30th November 1742.

Sarah BEASEMAN daughter of foresaid William BEASEMAN and Ruth was born 28th January 1744.

Katharine BEASEMAN daughter of foresaid William BEASEMAN and Ruth was born 27th July 1746.

William BEASESMAN son of William BEASEMAN and Ruth his wife was born 4th June 1748.

Sydney Ann HAMILTON daughter of John HAMILTON and Sydney his wife was born the 26 September 1750.

Thomas GIST son of William GIST and Violetta his wife was born the 19th day of May (twin) 1750.

Elizabeth GIST daughter of the aforesaid was born 19th of May (twin) 1759.

William New JURDIN son of Robert JURDIN and Ann his wife was born the 11 day of April 1750.

Sarah BAILEY daughter of George BAILEY and Mary his wife was born the 10th December 1749.

Sarah ELLIS daughter of Jane ELLIS was born the 14th day November, 1750.

Benjamin OGG son of George OGG, Junr. and Hellin his wife was born 29 April, 1748.

John HAWKINS son of Joseph HAWKINS and Elizabeth his wife was born 23 December 1713.

Mary SIMKIN daughter of John SIMKIN and Priscilla his wife was born 6 August 1716.

Augustine HAWKINS son of Joseph HAWKINS and Elizabeth his wife was born the 15th April 1721.

Delila BAKER daughter of Indimeon BAKER and Katherine his wife was born 14 November 1738.

Moses BAKER son of aforesaid Indimeon BAKER and Katherine his wife born 19th March 1740.

Rachel BAKER daughter of said Indimeon and Katherine BAKER his wife was born 24th January 1742.

Sarah BAKER daugher of said Indimeon and Katherine BAKER his wife was born 16th August 1744.

Margaret BAKER daughter of said Indimeon and Katherine BAKER his
wife was born 13th December 1747.
Indimeon BAKER son of the foresaid Indimeon BAKER and Katherine
his wife was born 19th July 1750.

Betty HAMMOND daughter of Lawrence HAMMOND and Abrilla his wife
was born 8th February 1748.

John SIMKIN son of John SIMKIN and Mary his wife was born 25th
December 1746.
Susannah SIMKIN daughter of the foresaid John SIMKIN and Mary was
born 2nd February 1748.
Priscilla SIMKIN daughter of the foresaid John SIMKIN and Mary
born 29 December 1750.

Rebecca FORD daughter of John FORD and Ruhamah his wife, born the
6th March 1750.

Benjamin BOND son of Peter BOND and Susannah his wife born the
22nd September 1750.

Benjamin MURPHEY son of William MURPHEY and Persila his wife born
the 16th July 1750.

Rachel GIST daughter of Thomas GIST and Sushanna his wife born
7th September 1750.

Archibal OWINGS son of Richard OWINGS and Ann his wife born the
2nd day of March 1750.

Stephen OWINGS son of Stephen OWINGS and Sarah his wife born
24th June 1750.

Ann ORRICK daughter of Nicholas ORRICK and Hannah his wife born
December 16th 1750.

Philip PINDELL son of John PINDELL and Elenor his wife born the
29th of March, 1752.

James PLOWMAN son of Jonathan PLOWMAN and Elizabeth his wife born
the 24th September 1751.

Greenberry OWINGS son of Richard OWINGS and Ann his wife born the
13th of April 1752.

Thomas CRADOCK son of Thomas CRADOCK and Katharine his wife born
May 30th 1752.

Hannah HAMILTON daughter of John HAMILTON and Sydney his wife
born 9th May 1752.

Shadrick BOND son of Richard BOND and Mary his wife born October
28th 1751.

John Eager HOWARD son of Cornelius HOWARD and Ruth his wife born 4th June 1752.

Nicholas HAWKINS son of John HAWKINS and Mary his wife was born 28th March 1753.

William GARDNER son of William GARDNER and Sarah his wife born the 8th January 1753.

David GIST son of Thomas GIST and Susannah his wife born the 29th April 1753.

Ann PEMBURTON daughter of Henry PEMBURTON and Margaret his wife born the 1st May 1746.

Phebey BOND daughter of Richard BOND and Mary his wife born October 23rd 1753.

Henry BOND son of Peter BOND and Susana his wife born April 22nd 1753.

Joshua GILL son of John GILL and Mary his wife born the 7th July 1753.

John PINDLE son of John PINDLE and Elenor his wife born the 6th February 1754.

Charles BARDELL son of Joseph and Jane BARDELL was born 24th January 1751.

Arthur CHENOWETH son of Arthur CHENOWETH and Sufirah his wife was born the 31st day of March 1740.
Hanah CHENOWETH daughter of Arthur CHENOWETH and Sufirah his wife was born the 20th day of November 1742.
John CHENOWETH son of Arthur CHENOWETH and Sufirah his wife born the 1st Day July 1745.
Samuel CHENOWETH son of Arthur CHENOWETH and Sufirah his wife was born the 1st day of December 1747.
William CHENOWETH son of Arthur CHENOWETH and Sufirah his wife was born the 29th July 1750.
Thomas CHENOWETH son of Arthur CHENOWETH and Sufirah his wife born the 21st day of March 1753.

William CARTER son of John CARTER and Francis his wife born the 2nd July 1748.
Mary CARTER daughter of John CARTER and Francis his wife born January 18th 1751.

Sarah CARTER daughter of John CARTER and Francis his wife born February 25th 1753.

Jonathan PLOWMAN son of Jonathan PLOWMAN and Elizabeth his wife was born the 13th of February 1754.

BIRTHS

Cornelius HOWARD son of Cornelius HOWARD and Ruth his wife born the 2nd day December 1754.

Elizabeth Rogers GILL daughter of John GILL and Mary his wife born the 13th June 1755.

John GIST son of William GIST and Violata his wife born 26th July 1752.
Violata GIST daughter of William GIST and Violata his wife born 13th March 1755.

Rebekah OWINGS daughter of Samuel OWINGS and Urath his wife born 21st October 1755.

John MOTHERBY son of Charles MOTHERBY and Ann his wife born the fifth day of August 1747.
Elizbeth MOTHERBY daughter of Charles MOTHERBY and Ann his wife was born the 23rd of May 1749.

Sarah BOND daughter of Richard BOND and Mary his wife born 23rd of December 1755.

Joseph CORNELIUS son of John CORNELIUS and Elenor his wife was born the 15th September 1752.
William CORNELIUS son of John CORNELIUS and Elenor his wife was born the 15th February 1754.
John CORNELIUS son of John CORNELIUS and Elenor his wife was born the 25th May 1756.
James HOWARD son of Cornelius HOWARD and Elenor his wife was born the 8th July 1757.

Ellen GIST daughter of William GIST and Violata his wife was born the 26th September 1757.

Richard FORTT son of Samuel FORTT and Susanna his wife was born the 14th August 1739.
Elizabeth FORTT daughter of Samuel FORTT and Susanna his wife was born the 2nd October 1741.
Samuel FORTT son of Samuel FORTT and Susanna his wife was born the 15th November 1743.

Henry BRAMWELL son of George BRAMWELL and Susanna his wife was born the 11th July 1751.
Mary BRAMWELL daughter of George BRAMWELL and Susanna his wife was born the 3rd May 1757.

Ann CRADOCK daughter of the Rev. Mr. Thomas CRADOCK and his Lady Katharine was born the 21st February 1755.

Thomas COCKEY son of John COCKEY and Elizabeth his wife was born the 24th December 1724.

Prudence GILL daughter of Stephen GILL and Elizabeth his wife was born the 6th February 1727.

Thomas COCKEY son of Thomas COCKEY and Prudence his wife was born the 15th April 1754.

Achsah COCKEY daughter of said Thomas COCKEY and Prudence his wife was born the 16th October 1755.

Elizabeth COCKEY daughter of said Thomas COCKEY and Prudence his wife was born the 18th April 1757.

Hellen BOND daughter of Richard BOND and Mary his wife was born the 13th January 1758.

John Howard FORD son of John FORD and Huhannah his wife was born 30th July 1753.

Joshua FORD son of said John FORD and Huhannah his wife was born the 23rd February 1756.

Eleanor FORD daughter of said John FORD and Huhannah his wife was born the 13th April 1758.

Christopher BOND son of Peter BOND and Susanna his wife was born the 2nd November 1757.

Nicholas Norman HARVEY son of Thomas HARVEY and Cassandra his wife was born the 26th November 1757.

Richard PLOWMAN son of Jonathan PLOWMAN and Elizabeth his wife was born the 23rd December 1756.

Edward PLOWMAN son of Jonathan PLOWMAN and Elizabeth his wife was born the 12th March 1759.

Urath COCKEY daughter of Edward COCKEY and Eleanor his wife was born the 27th April 1754.

Joshua COCKEY son of Edward COCKEY and Eleanor his wife was born the 20th October 1755.

William COCKEY son of Edward COCKEY and Eleanor his wife was born the 21st May 1758.

Nicholas RANDALL son of William RANDALL and Constant his wife was born the 2nd May 1759.

Margaret HARVEY daughter of Thomas HARVEY and Cassandra his wife was born the 13th June 1759.

Katharine PINDELL daughter of John PINDELL and Eleanor his wife was born the 13th September 1759.

Katharine GILL daughter of John GILL, Junr. and Sarah his wife was born the 19th July 1759.

Henry WELLS son of Alexander WELLS and Leah his wife was born the 7th September 1754.

Alexander WELLS son of Alexander WELLS and Leah his wife was born the 6th March 1756.

Anne WELLS daugher of Alexander WELLS and Leah his wife was born the 12th January 1758.

Michael WELLS daughter of Alexander WELLS and Leah his wife was born the 12th March 1759.

Elizabeth CARTER daughter of John CARTER and Frances his wife was born the 4th April 1756.

John BOWEN son of Solomon BOWEN and Temperance his wife was born the 7th October 1752.

Solomon BOWEN son of said Solomon BOWEN and Temperance his wife was born the 22nd March 1754.

Ruth BOWEN daughter of said Solomon BOWEN and Temperance his wife was born the 4th February 1756.

Naomi BOWEN daughter of said Solomon BOWEN and Temperance his wife was born the 15th March 1758.

Benjamin BOWEN son of said Solomon BOWEN and Temperance his wife was born the 12th March 1760.

Margaret BOND daughter of Richard BOND and Mary his wife was born the 2nd May 1760.

Joseph HUDGELL son of Thomas HUDGELL and Alice his wife was born the 22nd May 1746.

Elizabeth HUDGELL daughter of said Thomas HUDGELL and Alice his wife was born the 12th August 1748.

Ann HUDGELL daughter of Thomas HUDGELL and Alice his wife was born the 9th December 1750.

Thomas HUDGELL son of said Thomas HUDGELL and Alice his wife was born the 16th day of July 1752.

Henry HUDGELL son of said Thomas HUDGELL and Alice his wife was born the 29th day of January 1755.

Rosehannah HUDGELL daughter of said Thomas HUDGELL and Alice his wife was born the 29th day of July 1758.

Violetta HOWARD daughter of Cornelius HOWARD and Ruth his wife was born the 22nd day of September 1759.

Joshua CORNELIUS son of John CORNELIUS and Eleanor his wife was born the 26th day of December 1758.

Sarah HARVEY daughter of Thomas HARVEY and Cassandra his wife was born the 5th day of January 1761.

Nathaniel WELLS son of Alexander WELLS and Leah his wife was born the 1st day of April 1761.

Elizabeth WORTHINGTON daughter of Vachel WORTHINGTON and Priscilla his wife was born the 25th day of November 1759.

John COCKEY son of Thomas COCKEY and Prudence his wife was born the 20th of December 1758.

Anne COCKEY daughter of said Thomas COCKEY and Prudence his wife was born the 29th day of April 1760.

Charles COCKEY son of said Thomas COCKEY and Prudence his wife was born the 14th day of February 1762.

Katherine RISTEAU daughter of George RISTEAU and Frances his wife was born the 17th day of June 1758.

Eleanor RISTEAU daughter of said George RISTEAU and Frances his wife was born the 15th day of January 1760.

Elizabeth SHOWEL daughter of Thomas Roades SHOWEL and Phyllis Anna his wife was born the 6th day of November 1761.

Thomas JORDAN son of Robert JORDAN and Anne his wife was born the 20th October 1752.

Elizabeth JORDAN daughter of said Robert JORDAN and Anne his wife was born the 7th January 1755.

Richard New JORDAN son of said Robert JORDAN and Anne his wife was born the 19th February 1757.

John JORDAN son of said Richard JORDAN and Anne his wife was born the 20th January 1759.

Ruth JORDAN daughter of said Robert JORDAN and Anne his wife was born 22nd May 1761.

James MAJORS son of Esther MAJORS was born 9th April 1752.

Cornelius ORGAN son of William ORGAN and Esther his wife was born the 25th September 1754.

William ORGAN son of said William ORGAN and Esther his wife was born the 25th August 1757.

Eleanor ORGAN daughter of said William ORGAN and Esther his wife was born the 14th April 1760.

Thomas HARVEY son of Thomas HARVEY and Cassandra his wife was born the 24th May 1762.

Joshua BOND son of Peter BOND and Susanna his wife was born the 25th October 1759.

Susanna BOND daughter of said Peter BOND and Susanna his wife was born the 1st August 1762.

Elizabeth GOTT daughter of Richard GOTT and Ruth his wife was born the 22nd January 1759(7?).

Eleanor GOTT daughter of said Richard GOTT and Ruth his wife was born the 21st June 1760.

Richard GOTT son of said Richard and Ruth his wife was born 6th January 1761.

Joseph CURTIS son of Daniel CURTIS and Rachel his wife was born the 17th August 1759(7?).

Hannah CURTIS daughter of said Daniel CURTIS and Rachel his wife was born the 15th June 1761.

Mary PINDELL daughter of John PINDELL and Eleanor his wife was born the 22nd June 1761.

Ann CHENEY daughter of Benjamin Burgess CHENEY and Margaret his wife was born the 23rd November 1756.

Ruth CHENEY daughter of said Benjamin Burgess CHENRY and Margaret his wife was born the 11th April 1758.

BIRTHS

Adam CHENEY son of said Benjamin Burgess CHENEY and Margaret his
wife was born the 5th August 1759.
Rachel CHENEY daughter of said Benjamin Burgess CHENEY and
Margaret his wife was born the 18th December 1761.

Sarah GOTT daughter of Richard GOTT and Elizabeth his wife was
born the 30th December 1750.
Rachel GOTT daughter of said Richard GOTT and Elizabeth his wife
was born the 3rd day of May 1754.

Samuel CORNELIUS son of John CORNELIUS and Eleanor his wife was
born the 28th day of May 1761.

Francis AIRS son of John AIRS and Elizabeth his wife was born the
14th day of October 1762.

Philip HOWARD son of Cornelius HOWARD and Ruth his wife was born
the 17th September 1762.

John BANKS son of John BANKS and Mary his wife was born the 7th
October 1757.
James BANKS son of said John BANKS and Mary his wife was born the
5th May 1759.
Elizabeth BANKS daughter of said John BANKS and Mary his wife was
born the 8th February 1761.
William BANKS son of said John BANKS and Mary his wife was born
the 14th January 1763.

Henry WORREL son of Henry WORREL and Julaitha his wife was born
the 19(7?)th January 1747.
Thomas WORREL son of said Henry WORREL and Julaitha his wife was
born the 15th December 1749.
John WORREL son of said Henry WORREL and Julaitha his wife was
born the 13th March 1752.

Julaitha WORREL daughter of Henry WORREL and Rachel his wife was
born the 22nd September 1754.
Elizabeth WORREL daughter of said Henry WORREL and Rachel his
wife was born the 21st May 1756.
Mary WORREL daughter of said Henry WORREL and Rachel his wife was
born the 25th November 1757.
Amon WORREL son of said Henry WORREL and Rachel his wife was born
the 5th December 1759.
Hannah WORREL daughter of said Henry WORREL and Rachel his wife
was born the 19th July 1762.

Edmund FORD son of John FORD and Huhannah his wife was born the
2nd August 1760.

John GILL son of John GILL, Junr. and Sarah his wife was born the
10th December 1762.

John Elder GIST son of Joseph GIST and Elizabeth his wife was
born the 2nd January 1761.

Cecil GIST daughter of said Joseph GIST and Elizabeth his wife was born the 12th November 1762.

Thomas RISTEAU son of George RISTEAU and Frances his wife was born the 16th January 1763.

Hannah CROSS daughter of Robert CROSS and Jermima his wife was born the 24th March 1754.

Nicodemus CROSS son of said Robert CROSS and Jermima his wife was born the 19th July 1758.

Benjamin CROSS son of said Robert CROSS and Jermima his wife was born the 23rd April 1760.

Anne CROSS daughter of said Robert CROSS and Jemima his wife was born the 13th January 1763.

Elizabeth GILL daughter of William GILL and Ruth his wife was born the 30th January 1762.

John GILL son of said William GILL and Ruth his wife was born the 20th May 1763.

Joshua CONSTANTINE son of Patrick CONSTANTINE and Anne his wife was born the 3rd December 1760.

Daniel CONSTANTINE son of said Patrick CONSTANTINE and Anne his wife was born the 4th December 1762.

Thomas TOWSON son of Thomas TOWSON and Elizabeth his wife was born the 25th April 1752.

Sarah TOWSON daughter of said Thomas TOWSON and Elizabeth his wife was born 18th January 1754.

Joshua TOWSON son of said Thomas TOWSON and Elizabeth his wife was born the 18th January 1756.

Hannah TOWSON daughter of said Thomas TOWSON and Elizabeth his wife was born the 23rd October 1758.

James TOWSON son of said Thomas TOWSON and Elizabeth his wife was born the 21st September 1760.

Shadrach TOWSON son of said Thomas TOWSON and Elizabeth his wife was born the 3rd September 1762.

Henry BUTLER son of Amon BUTLER and Elizabeth his wife was born the 13th April 1746.

Nicholas BUTLER son of said Amon BUTLER and Elizabeth his wife was born the 13th April 1746.

Amon BUTLER son of said Amon BUTLER and Elizabeth his wife was born the 24th December 1750.

Ruth BUTLER daughter of said Amon BUTLER and Elizabeth his wife was born the 23rd February 1753.

Absalom BUTLER son of said Amon BUTLER and Elizabeth his wife was born the 8th September 1758.

Elizabeth BUTLER daughter of said Amon BUTLER and Elizabeth his wife was born 23rd January 1760.

Joseph BUTLER son of said Amon BUTLER and Elizabeth his wife was born the 14th May 1763.

Bezaleel WELLS son of Alexander WELLS and Leah his wife was born the 28th January 1763.

BIRTHS

Stephen COCKEY son of Thomas COCKEY and Prudence his wife was born the 23rd January 1764.

Thomas PINDELL son of John PINDELL and Eleanor his wife was born the 1st August 1763.

William JONES son of Benjamin JONES and Honor his wife was born the 27th January 1762.
Patience JONES daughter of said Benjamin JONES and Honor his wife was born the 24th July 1763.

Isaac BLISSARD son of William BLISSARD and Luranah his wife was born the 19th May 1751.
John BLISSARD son of said William BLISSARD and Luranah his wife was born the 3rd September 1755.

Greenbury BAXTER son of John BAXTER and Mary his wife was born the 4th October 1735.
John BAXTER son of said John BAXTER by Mary his said wife was born the 15th April 1738.
Mary BAXTER daughter of said John BAXTER and Mary his second wife was born 17th November 1742.
Phillis Anna BAXTER daughter of said John BAXTER and Mary his wife was born 26th February 1743.
Elizabeth BAXTER daughter of said John BAXTER and Mary his wife was born the 16th July 1745.
John BAXTER son of said John BAXTER and Mary his wife was born the 17th February 1746.
Edmund BAXTER son of said John BAXTER and Mary his wife was born the 28th November 1748.
George BAXTER son of said John BAXTER and Mary his wife was born the 31st January 1751.
Benjamin BAXTER son of said John BAXTER and Mary his wife was born the 21st May 1753.
Bethuel BAXTER son of said John BAXTER and Mary his wife was born the 6th March 1755.
William BAXTER son of said John BAXTER and Mary his wife was born the 18th April 1757.

William BUTLER son of Absalom BUTLER and Mary his wife was born the 3rd March 1752.

Thomas BARNEY son of Moses BARNEY and Sarah his wife was born the 19th July 1759.

Benjamin BARNEY son of said Moses BARNEY and Sarah his wife was born the 17th January 1761.
Anne BARNEY daughter of the said Moses BARNEY and Sarah his wife was born the 9th December 1762.

William HUDSON son of Thomas HUDSON and Elizabeth his wife was born the 8th October 1746.
Mary HUDSON daughter of said Thomas HUDSON and Elizabeth his wife was born the 9th September 1748.

Sarah HUDSON daughter of said Thomas HUDSON and Elizabeth his
wife was born the 24th December 1750.
Thomas HUDSON son of said Thomas HUDSON and Elizabeth his wife
was born the 15th March 1752.
Joshua HUDSON son of said Thomas HUDSON and Elizabeth his wife
was born the 16th September 1756.
Margaret HUDSON daughter of said Thomas HUDSON and Elizabeth his
wife was born the 10th May 1759.
Daniel HUSDON son of said Thomas HUDSON and Elizabeth his wife
was born the 30th May 1761.

Mary GOTT daughter of Richard GOTT and Ruth his wife was born the
30th March 1764.

John KELLEY son of James KELLEY and Prudence his wife was born
the 10th April 1750.
Eleanor KELLEY daughter of said James KELLEY and Prudence his
wife was born the 4th July 1752.
Charles KELLEY son of said James KELLEY and Prudence his wife was
born the 4th August 1754.
Susanna KELLEY daughter of said James KELLEY and Prudence his
wife was born the 19th June 1756.
Ann KELLEY daughter of said James KELLEY and Prudence his wife
was born the 5th May 1758.
Thomas Deye KELLEY son of said James KELLEY and Prudence his wife
was born the 13th July 1760.

Honor JONES daughter of Benjamin JONES and Honor his wife was
born the 24th January 1765.

Rebecca OSBORNE daughter of Joseph OSBORNE and Urath his wife was
born the 30th October 1761.
Urath Karenhappuch OSBORNE daughter of said Joseph OSBORNE and
Urath his wife was born 11th of March 1763.

John RISTEAU son of George RISTEAU and Frances his wife was born
the 14th of April 1765.

Charles GILL son of John GILL, Junr. and Sarah his wife was born
the 27th April 1764.

Ely MILLER son of Joseph MILLER and Mary his wife was born the
27th October 1760.
Rachel MILLER daughter of said Joseph MILLER and Mary his wife
was born the 5th August 1762.
George MILLER son of said Joseph MILLER and Mary his wife was
born the 25th September 1764.

William HARVEY son of Thomas HARVEY and Cassandra his wife was
born the 22nd of December 1764.

Anne HOWARD daughter of Cornelius HOWARD and Ruth his wife was
born the 10th July 1765.

Sarah PINDELL daughter of John PINDELL and Eleanor his wife was born the 29th June 1765.

Ruth FORD daughter of Thomas FORD (son of John) & Elizabeth his wife was born the 12th October 1765.

Joseph GIST son of Joseph GIST and Elizabeth his wife was born the 12 day August 1764.
Jemima GIST daughter of the aforesaid Joseph GIST and Elizabeth his wife was born the 4th May 1766.

Charles CHAPMAN son of Luke CHAPMAN and Sophia his wife was born the 20th of October 1755.
Marget CHAPMAN daughter of the aforesaid Luke CHAPMAN and Sophia his wife was born 5th of March 1757.
Daniel CHAPMAN son of the aforesaid Luke CHAPMAN and Sophia his wife was born the 10th of November 1758.
Stephen CHAPMAN son of the aforesaid Luke CHAPMAN and Sophia his wife was born the 19th of January 1760.
Mary CHAPMAN daughter of the aforesaid Luke CHAPMAN and Sophia his wife was born the 13th of August 1761.
Sarah CHAPMAN daughter of Luke CHAPMAN and Sophia his wife was born the 20th of July 1763.
Leah CHAPMAN daughter of Luke CHAPMAN and Sophia his wife was born the 24th of May 1765.

Elizabeth HUTSON daughter of Thomas HUTSON and Elizabeth his wife was born the 25th of July 1766.

Elizabeth WELLS daughter of Francis WELLS and Ann his wife was born 4th of February 1758.
Robert Tevis WELLS son of Francis WELLS and Ann his wife was born 25th January 1759.
Marget WELLS daughter of Francis WELLS and Ann his wife was born the 30th January 1760.
Susannah WELLS daughter of Francis WELLS and Ann his wife was born the 2d of November 1761.
Thomas WELLS son of the aforesaid Francis WELLS and Ann his wife was born the 17th January 1763.
Joshua WELLS son of the aforesaid Francis WELLS and Ann his wife was born the 6th December 1764.
Sarah WELLS daughter of the aforesaid Francis WELLS and Ann his wife was born 22d August 1766.

Richard BOND son of Nicodemus BOND and Rachel his wife wasborn the 14th October 1765.

Ephraim CHAPMAN son of Luke CHAPMAN and Sophia his wife was born the 27th January 1767.

Thomas COCKEY son of Edward COCKEY and Eleanor his wife was born the 21st March 1762.

James WELLS son of John WELLS and Dinah his wife was born 25th January 1764.

Constant WELLS daughter to the aforesaid John WELLS and Dinah his wife was born the 26th May 1766.

Joshua Howard GIST son of Joseph GIST and Elisabeth his wife was born the 3rd day of March 1768.

Cassandra HARVEY daughter to Thomas HARVEY and Cassandra his wife was born the 12th of February 1767.

Leaven Lawrence OWINGS son of Thomas OWINGS and Ruth his wife was born the 14th of October 1761.
Samuel OWINGS son of Thomas OWINGS and Ruth his wife was born the 12th of June 1763.
Thomas OWINGS son of Thomas OWINGS and Ruth his wife was born the 7th day of July 1765.
Thomas Bale OWINGS son of Thomas OWINGS and Ruth his wife was born the 26th day of May 1767.

Michael ELDER son of John ELDER and Onner his wife, was born the 23rd November 1763.
Halen ELDER daughter to John ELDER and Onner his wife was born the 14th July 1765.
Providence ELDER daughter to John ELDER and Onner his wife was born 11th September 1767.

Frances RISTEAU daugher to George RISTEAU and Frances his wife was born the 26th July 1767.

Henry OWINGS son of Nathaniel OWINGS and Urath his wife was born the 15th October 1763.
Joshua OWINGS son of Nathaniel OWINGS and Urath his wife was born the 7th of November 1765.
Elizabeth OWINGS daughter to the aforesaid Nathaniel OWINGS and Urath his wife was born the 8th of December 1767.

Mary Lyon WILLIAMSON daughter of Alexander WILLIAMSON and Elizabeth his wife was born the 29th January at eight o'clock in the morning 1769.

Naomi WELLS daughter of Francis WELLS and Ann his wife was born the 3rd of February 1768.
Ruth WELLS daughter of the aforesaid Francis WELLS and Ann his wife was born the 7th of March 1769.
Ann WELLS daughter of Thomas WELLS and Elizabeth his wife was born the 11th of March 1756.

John CARTER son of John CARTER and Margaret his wife was born the 8th of November 1763.
Joshua CARTER son of John CARTER and Margaret his wife was born July 28th 1766.

Sophia CHAPMAN daughter of Luke CHAPMAN and Sophia his wife was born the 29th day of January 1769.

Ann WELLS daughter of Joseph WELLS and Susanah his wife was born
March 29th 1762.
Thomas WELLS son of Joseph WELLS and Susanah his wife was born
August 31st 1766.
Marget WELLS daughter of Joseph WELLS and Susanah his wife was
born April 13, 1765.
Susanah WELLS daughter of Joseph WELLS and Susanah his wife was
born November 19th 1769.

Francis WELLS son of Thomas WELLS and Elizabeth his wife was born
born June 26th 1737.
Joseph WELLS son of Thomas WELLS and Elizabeth his wife was born
May 29th 1739.
John WELLS son of Thomas WELLS and Elizabeth his wife was born
March 25th 1743.

James WELLS son of Thomas WELLS and Elizabeth his wife was born
November 5th 1747.
Thomas WELLS son of Thomas WELLS and Elizabeth his wife was born
August 9th 1750.
Richard WELLS son of Thomas WELLS and Elizabeth his wife was born
June 30th 1753.

Elizabeth HOWARD daughter of Joshua HOWARD and Johanah his wife
was born April 27th 1714.

George Howard ELDER son of Charles ELDER and Ruth his wife was
born March 1st 1770.

Terrishu ELDER daughter of Owen ELDER and Nancy his wife was born
January 12th 1767.
Ruth ELDER daughter of Owen ELDER and Nancy his wife was born
March 6th 1769.

Cornelius Howard GIST son of Joseph GIST and Elizabeth his wife
was born the 25th of January 1770.

Samuel CHAPMAN son of Luke CHAPMAN and Sophia his wife was born
the 9th day of November 1770.

Richard HARVEY son of Thomas HARVEY and Cassandra his wife was
born the 24th day of September 1770.

Rebeccah RISTEAU daughter to George RISTEAU and Frances his wife
was born the 5th day December 1770.

Samuel DORSEY son of Nicholas DORSEY, Jurn. and Ruth his wife was
born the 17th of November 1765.
Nancy DORSEY daughter of the aforesaid Nicholas DORSEY, Junr. and
Ruth his wife was born the 20th day of July 1768.
Josiah DORSEY son of the aforesaid Nicholas Dorsey, Junr. and
Ruth his wife was born the 11th day of May 1770.

John ELDER, Junr. son of John ELDER and Sarah his wife was born June the 5th 1772.

Violata GIST daughter of Joseph GIST and Elizabeth his wife was born June 6th at ten o'clock in the morning - twin 1772.
William GIST son of the aforesaid Joseph GIST and Elizabeth his wife was born June 6th 1772 about six o'clock in the afternoon- twin.

Robert North CARNAN son of Christopher CARNAN and Elizabeth his wife was born the 8th of August at 9 o'clock at night 1756.

John Owen ELDER son of Owen ELDER and Nancy his wife was born the 19th of February 1771.

Thomas Cradock WALKER son of Charles WALKER and Ann his wife was born on Wednesday the 16th of June at 3 o'clock in the morning, 1773.

Caleb WORRELL son of Henry WORRELL and Rachel his wife was born the 9th of July 1765.
Jessy WORRELL son of Henry WORREL and Rachel his wife was born November 15th 1770.

John BROWN son of John BROWN and Katherine his wife was born in May 1759.

David BROWN son of David BROWN and Naomi his wife was born December 3rd 1763.

Elizabeth GIST daughter of Joseph GIST and Elizabeth his wife was born March 21st 1774.

Ruth MILLER daughter of Joseph MILLER and Mary his wife was born the last day of August 1765.
Elijah MILLER son of Joseph MILLER and Mary his wife was born the 7th of April 1768.

Elizabeth HARVEY daughter of Thomas HARVEY and Cassandra his wife was born March 17th 1772.

William CALHOUN son of James CALHOUN and Ann his wife was born November 30th about 8 o'clock at night 1767.
James CALHOUN son of James CALHOUN and Ann his wife was born November 4th about 8 o'clock in the morning 1770.
Elizabeth CALHOUN daughter of James CALHOUN and Ann his wife was born the 26th of April, about 4 o'clock in the morning, 1774.

Samuel LAWRENCE son of Benjamin LAWRENCE and Urath his wife was born September the 28th 1764.
Polly LAWRENCE daughter of Benjamin LAWRENCE and Urath his wife was born the 28th of February 1767.
Susanna LAWRENCE daughter of Benjamin LAWRENCE and Urath his wife was born the 4th of May 1769.

Rebeccah LAWRENCE daughter of Benjamin LAWRENCE and Urath his wife was born the 4th of July 1771.

Leaven LAWRENCE son of Benjamin LAWRENCE and Urath his wife was born the 8th of April 1774.

Susana WALKER daughter of Charles WALKER and Ann his wife was born on Sunday the 3rd of September 1775.

Rebecca CARNAN daughter of Charles CARNAN and Mary his wife was born June the 8th 1775.

James GIST son of Joseph GIST and Elizabeth his wife was born February 20th 1776.

Henry BOIM (?) son of Mary BOIM was born December the 27th 1775.

Mary CRADOCK daughter of John CRADOCK and Ann his wife was born the 27th of February 1778.

Owen GIST son of Joseph GIST and Elizabeth his wife was born the 9th of January 1778.

Jemima ELDER daughter of John ELDER and Sarah his wife was born March the 1st 1774.

Onour ELDER daughter of John ELDER and Sarah his wife was born February 21st, 1776.

Owen ELDER son of John ELDER and Sarah is wife was born May the 9th 1778.

Katharine CRADOCK daughter of John CRADOCK and Ann his wife was born December 5th 1779.

Frances Todd CARNAN daughter of Robert Nth. CARNAN and Katharine his wife was born November 24th 1777.

Chistropher CARNAN son of Robert N. CARNAN and Katharine his wife was born the 19th of July 1780.

James WALKER son of Charles WALKER and Ann his wife was born Tuesday March the 11th 1777.

Katharine WALKER daughter of Charles WALKER and Ann his wife was born January 6th 1779.

Elizabeth Hulse WALKER daughter of Charles WALKER and Ann his wife was born December 10th 1780.

Arthur CRADOCK son of John CRADOCK and Ann his wife was born April 17th 1782.

Agnes Ann WALKER daughter of Charles WALKER and Ann his wife was born February 22nd 1783.

Elizabeth CRADOCK daughter of John CRADOCK and Ann his wife was born October 9th 1784.

Ann CRADOCK daughter of John CRADOCK and Ann his wife was born 1786.

Margaret Mary WALKER daughter of Charles WALKER and Ann his wife was born 2nd April 1785.

John George WALKER son of Charles WALKER and Ann his wife was born 6th July 1787.

Sarah WALKER daughter of Charles WALKER and Ann his wife born 21st June 1790.

Frances WALKER daughter of Charles WALKER and Ann his wife born 22nd March 1792.

JAMES HOWARD REGISTER

Charles GORSUCH son of Norman and Keturah GORSUCH born the 20th August 1791, baptized 30th April 1792 by the Rev. John Coleman.

Andrew JONES son of Joshua and Mary JONES born the 21st December 1791, baptized 30th April 1792 by the Rev. John Coleman.

Susana TIVIS (TIVES?) daughter of Benjamin and Ellen TIVES born the 12th February 1792, baptized 1st May 1792 by the Rev. Mr. Bend.

Harriot BROWN daughter of David and Jemima BROWN born 1st November 1791, baptized 1st May 1792 by the Rev. Mr. Bend.

Keturah Ann WHITE daughter of Richard and Elizabeth WHITE born 8th November 1791, baptized 1st May 1792 by the Rev. Mr. Bend.
Ruth WHITE daughter of above and bapitzied as above, born 30th May 1789.

Stephen HILL son of Thomas and Actia HILL born June 12th 1791, baptized 1st May 1792 by the Rev. Mr. Bend.

John BEASEMAN son of George and Sally BEASEMAN born October 4th 1791, baptized 1st May 1792 by the Rev. Mr. Bend.

Frances WALKER daughter of Charles and Ann WALKER born 22nd March 1792, baptized 28th May 1792 by the Rev. Mr. Bend.

Stephen BROWN son of Elias and Ann BROWN born 4th April 1791, baptized 28th May 1792 by the Rev. Mr. Bend.

Jeremiah Heighe JOHNSON son of Jeremiah and Eleanor JOHNSON born September 1788, baptized 28th May 1792 by the Rev. Mr. Bend.

John DURNAY son of James and Anne DURNAY born 8th May 1792, baptized the 28th May 1792 by the Rev. Mr. Bend.

Daniel slave of Eleanor CROXALL aged 45 years, baptized the 16th August 1792 by the Rev. Mr. Bend.

Michael GLADMAN son of Thomas and Eleanor GLADMAN born 4th August 1792, baptized by the Rev. Mr. Oliver, 3rd June 1793.

Elias BROWN son of Elias and Ann BROWN born 9th May 1793, baptized by the Rev. Mr. Oliver 15th June 1793.

Thomas GORE born May 3rd, 1785; Elizabeth GORE born July 11, 1787, Anna GORE born March 11, 1792; all children of Andrew and Sarah GORE, baptized by the Rev. Mr. Oliver 15th June 1793.

William Gustavus KELLEY son of Patrick and Ariana KELLEY born 10th December 1792, baptized by the Rev. Mr. Oliver 16th June 1793.

Pamelia GLOVER daughter of Josh. & Rachel GLOVER born 26th July 1792, baptized by the Rev. Mr. Oliver 16th June 1793.

Denton SHIPLEY son of William and Susana SHIPLEY born 15th November 1792, baptized by the Rev. Mr. Oliver 16th June 1793.

John SHIPLEY, 3 years old, Bale SHIPLEY, 5 years old; sons of Benjamin and Elizabeth SHIPLEY baptized 16th June 1793.

John Talbott RISTEAU son of John Talbott RISTEAU and Elizabeth his wife born 22nd February 1793, baptized 4th August 1793.

Joshua DEEMS son of John and Patience DEEMS baptized 15th September 1793, aged 15 months.

William Cradock WALKER son of Charles and Ann WALKER born 11th February 1798, baptized 8th June 1798.

Arrebella STARR daughter of James and Ann STARR was born 21st September 1793 baptized by the Rev. Mr. Oliver 24th November 1793.
James Tod STARR son of James and Ann STARR was born in the year 1795, baptized 7th April 1799 by Rev. Mr. Coleman.
Dorcas Grover STARR daughter of James and Ann STARR was born 31st January 1798, baptized 7th April 1799 by Rev. Mr. Coleman.

Matilda OWINGS daughter of Thomas and Ruth OWINGS was born 7th of October 1789, baptized 7th April 1790 by Rev. Mr. Coleman.

John Cradock CROMWELL son of Stephen and Mary CROMWELL his wife was born 14th November 1798, baptized 7th April 1799 By Rev. Mr. Coleman.

Betsy OWINGS daughter of Thomas and Ruth OWINGS was born 30th of April 1769.
Isaac OWINGS son to ditto born 9th April 1771.
David OWINGS son to ditto born 8th April 1773.
Susanna OWINGS daughter to ditto born 27th June 1775.
Ruth OWINGS daughter to ditto born 31st July 1777.
Jesse OWINGS son to ditto born 14th September 1779.
Anne OWINGS daughter to ditto born 4th November 1781.
Leve OWINGS son to ditto born 10th June 1784.
Harod OWINGS son to ditto born 2nd October 1786.

Anna Maria GOTT daughter of Richard GOTT and Ruth was born June 9th, 1797; baptized 13th May 1799 by Rev. John Coleman.

Samuel Norwood GOTT son of Richard GOTT and Ruth his wife born November 4th 1798, baptized 13th May 1799 by Rev. John Coleman.

Garrett Garrettson WORTHINGTON son of Samuel WORTHINGTON and Martha his wife born February 19th 1797, baptized 26th May 1799 by Rev. John Coleman.

Violetta Elizabeth ELDER daughter of Charles ELDER and Sally his wife born the 22nd April 1799, baptized 5th August 1799 by Rev. Mr. Coleman.

Sidney RITTER daughter of Thomas and Elizabeth RITTER born 1st December 1798 baptized the 1st September by Rev. Mr. Coleman 1799.

Sarah HOOK daughter of Jacob and Elizabeth HOOK born 20th November 1798 baptized by the Rev. Mr. Coleman 1st September 1799.

George MASON son of Michael MASON and Catharine his wife born 16th May 1799, baptized by Rev. Mr. Coleman 1st September 1799.

Anna MASON daughter of Michael and Elizabeth MASON born 27th August 1797 baptized by Rev. Mr. Coleman 1st September 1799.

Rebecca LEAF daughter of John and Rachel LEAF born 27th January 1798, baptized by Rev. Mr. Coleman 1st September 1799.

Thomas BAILEY son of John and Rebecca BAILEY born 7th July 1798 baptized by Rev. Mr. Coleman 1st September 1799.

Ruth Edward STANSBURY daughter of John Ensor STANSBURY and Mary his wife born 15th September 1797, baptized 23rd September 1799 by the Rev. Mr. John Coleman.

James Edward STANSBURY born February 26th 1799 son of Abraham and Elizabeth STANSBURY baptized by the Rev. Mr. John Coleman 23rd September 1799.

James Howard MACKEY son of William and Ruth MACKEY born 12th June 1799, baptized 4th November 1799 by the Rev. Mr. Coleman.

Federal Anne Buonaparte GIST daughter of Joshua and Sarah GIST born 14th August 1799, baptized by the Rev. Mr. Coleman 4th November 1799.

William Lynch OWINGS son of Samuel and Ruth OWINGS born the 7th August 1799, baptized by the Rev. Mr. Coleman 17th November 1799.

William OWINGS son of Samuel and Deborah was born the 5th day of May 1767.
Urath OWINGS daughter of Samuel and Deborah OWINGS was born February 22nd 1769.

Samuel OWINGS son of Samuel OWINGS and Deborah OWINGS was born 3rd of April 1770.

Eleanor OWINGS daughter of Samuel and Deborah OWINGS was born 7th February 1772.

Sarah OWINGS daughter of Samuel and Deborah OWINGS was born 25th December 1773.

Rebecca OWINGS daughter of Samuel and Deborah OWINGS was born 12th January 1776.

Deborah OWINGS daughter of Samuel and Deborah OWINGS was born 14th November 1777.

Frances OWINGS daughter of Samuel and Deborah OWINGS was born 30th September 1779.

Rachel OWINGS daughter of Samuel and Deborah OWINGS was born 27th August 1781.

Mary OWINGS daughter of Samuel and Deborah OWINGS was born 27th March 1784.

Ann OWINGS daughter of Samuel and Deborah OWINGS was born 20th December 1785.

Beale OWINGS son of Samuel and Deborah OWINGS was born 17th November 1791.

Eliza OWINGS daughter of Beal and Ruth OWINGS born 25th August 1798 baptized by the Rev. Mr. Coleman 25th May 1800.

Mary FONDEY daughter of Abraham and Margaret FONDEY born 15th August 1799, baptized by the Rev. Mr. Coleman 25th May 1800.

Joshua BROWN son of Joshua and Mary BROWN born 15th June 1799, baptized by the Rev. Mr. Coleman 25th May 1800.

James HARP son of Frederick and Mary HARP born 18th September 1799, baptized by the Rev. Mr. Coleman 25th May 1800.

Ann GLADMAN daughter of Michael and Rebecca GLADMAN born 2nd February 1798, baptized by the Rev. Mr. Coleman 25th May 1800.

Elizabeth Ann CARR daughter of Daniel and Susanna CARR born 25th November 1799, baptized by the Rev. Mr. Coleman 25th May 1800.

Prudence Ann BROWN daughter of Elias and Ann BROWN born 21 April 1799, baptized by the Rev. Mr. Coleman 25th May 1800.

Patience L. DORSEY daughter of Edward and Susanna DORSEY born 23rd April 1788, baptized by the Rev. Mr. Coleman 16th December 1800.

Leaven L. DORSEY son of Edward and Susanna DORSEY was born 19th December 1799, baptized by the Rev. Mr. Coleman 16th December 1800.

Cecelia LOUDERSLAGER daughter of Solomon and Anne LOUDERSLAGER born 26th September 1800, baptized by the Rev. Mr. Coleman 30th November 1800.

Eleanor Caroline JOHNSON daughter of Hickman JOHNSON and Ann his wife was born 26th May 1798, baptized by the Rev. Mr. Coleman February 13th 1801.

William Mc Langhlin RISTEAU son of John Talbott RISTEAU and Elizabeth his wife was born 18th February 1791, baptized by the Rev. Mr. Coleman 17th February 1801.

Thomas Cradock RISTEAU son of John Talbott RISTEAU and Elizabeth his wife was born 21st December 1795, baptized by the Rev. Mr. Coleman 17th February 1801.

Charles Walker RISTEAU son of John Talbott RISTEAU and Elizabeth his wife was born 14th July 1797, baptized by the Rev. Mr. Coleman 17th February 1801.

Robert Carnan RISTEAU son of John Talbott RISTEAU and Elizabeth his wife was born 2nd March 1799, baptized by the Rev. Mr. Coleman 17th February 1801.

Benjamin Denny RISTEAU son of John Talbott RISTEAU and Elizabeth his wife was born 24th November 1800, baptized by the Rev. Mr. Coleman 17th February 1801.

Dorothea BUCHANAN daughter of Andrew and Ann BUCHANAN his wife born December 30th 1800, baptized by the Rev. Mr. Coleman 6th August 1801.

Eliza Murray GILL daughter of Benjamin GILL and Jemima his wife born 17th September 1793.

Kezia Murray GILL daughter of Benjamin GILL and Jemima his wife born 26th November 1795.

Rachel Murray GILL daughter of Benjamin GILL and Jemima his wife born 9th April 1798.

Jabez Murray GILL son of Benjamin GILL and Jemima his wife born 17th August 1800.

Nancy Murray GILL daughter of Benjamin GILL and Jemima his wife born 21st May 1803.

JOSEPH WEST REGISTER

Elizabeth Digby Belcher eight weeks old and daughter of the Rev. Thomas Fitch OLIVER, Rector of St. Thomas's Parish, Baltimore County and Sarah his wife baptized June 27th 1795.

Eunice DORSEY 13 months old, daughter of Lloyd and Catharine DORSEY of Elk Ridge, baptized bythe Rev. Mr. Oliver, March 18th 1794.

Edward, born September 8th 1788; Amos born January 26, 1794: Children of Ormond and Hannah JARVIS, baptized by the Rev. Oliver, March 24th 1794.

Ele, aged five years, October 5th 1793; Rebecca, four years, March 28th 1794; Mercy two years, January 2, 1792(?); Mary born October 20th 1793: Children of Aquilla JARVIS and Eliza his wife, baptized by the Rev. Mr. Oliver, April 20th, 1794.

John born March 2nd 1794 son of John DEEMS and Patience his wife, baptized by the Rev. Mr. Oliver April 20th 1794.

John, three years old, July 1793; George, born January 27th 1794: Children of Thomas and Mary CRAMPTON, baptized by the Rev. Mr. Oliver, April 20th 1794.

Ruth born July 2nd 1792; Martha born November 9th 1793: Children of Stephen GARRETT and Priah GILL baptized by the Rev. Mr. Oliver, June 9th 1794.

Sybil West WALKER born January 9th 1794 daughter of Charles and Ann WALKER, baptized by the Rev. Mr. Oliver June 9th 1794.

Leah Ann born August 13th 1793 daughter of Francis and Sarah DINES, baptized by the Rev. Mr. Oliver, June 9th 1794.

Hannah MAYERS a free Mulatto born June 1790, daughter of Samuel and Jane MAYERS, baptized by the Rev. Mr. Oliver, June 9th 1794.

Nicholas Nathan (Black) belonging to Mr. Charles WALKER, born December 9th 1791, baptized byt he Rev. Mr. Oliver, June 9th 1794.

Anne aged 4 years, _____ aged 2 months: Children of Rachel HOOKER of Westminster, Frederick County, baptized by the Rev. Mr. Oliver June 21st 1794.

Ellen North aged 4 months and 21 days and daughter of Thomas and Eleanor MOALE of Baltimore, baptized by the Rev. Mr. Oliver, June 29th 1794.

John Sterrett born 12th March 1794 son of James and Harriett GITTINGS of Baltimore, baptized by the Rev. Mr. Oliver, June 30th 1794.

Michael 3 years old, first of June last Hannah 1 year old, 26th March last; Children of Robert and Mary ALDER, baptized by the Rev. Mr. Oliver, July 27th 1794.

Peregrine 3 years old; Samuel Christopher 12 months: Children of Beale and Ruth OWINGS, baptized by the Rev. Mr. Oliver September 21st 1794.

Polly 10 months old, daughter of Absolom and Providence SHIPLEY, baptized by the Rev. Mr. Oliver Septmber 21st 1794.

Othen son of Deborah and Joshua WILSON, baptized by the Rev. Mr. Oliver September 21st 1794.

Rebecca, 7 months old, daughter of James and Ann PORTER, baptized by the Rev. Mr. Oliver, September 21st 1794.

Nimrod, 5 years old; Henrietta, 10 months old: Children of Joshua DORSEY and _____ his wife, baptized by the Rev. Mr. Oliver, September 21st 1794.

James, nine months old, son of Robert and Sarah CUSHING, baptized by the Rev. Mr. Oliver, September 21st 1794.

William born February 8th, son of Morris and Keturah PETTICOAT, baptized by the Rev. Mr. Oliver, October 23rd 1794.

Elizabeth born April 22nd 1792; Thomas, born October 24th 1793: Children of Margaret PINDLE, baptized by the Rev. Mr. Oliver, October 23rd 1794.

Caleb born October 12th 1793, son of William and Mary GILL, baptized by the Rev. Mr. Oliver, October 23rd 1794.

Keturah born July 23rd 1790; Ruth born September 13th 1792: Children of Edward and Catharine BOND, baptized by the Rev. Mr. Oliver, October 23rd 1794.

William JARVIS (adult & clinic?) aged 14 years March 1794, baptized by the Rev. Mr. Oliver, November 15th 1794.

Elizabeth JOHNSON and William JOHNSON (adults); baptized by the Rev. Mr. Oliver, December 21st 1794.

Anna Maria, 10 weeks old, daughter of the Rev. J. G. J. BEND and Mary his wife, baptized at St. Paul's Church, Baltimore, whereof he is Rector, by the Rev. Mr. Oliver, December 27th 1794.

Nicholas son of John and Mary GILL, baptized by the Rev. Mr. Oliver February 19th 1795.

Absolom GILL born September 8th 1781; John GILL born May 28th 1783; William GILL born August 20th 1784: Children of Mary BARNEY; baptized by the Rev. Mr. Oliver February 19th 1795.

Andrew son of George and Letitia BUCHANAN born 179? at Baltimore, baptized by the Rev. Mr. Oliver, July 13th 1795.

Hannah daughter of Samuel and Ruth OWINGS born January 1794, baptized by the Rev. Mr. Oliver, August 2nd 1795.

Sarah daughter of Charles and Sarah CARNAN born April 20th 1795, baptized by the Rev. Mr. Oliver, September 6th 1795.

Sarah daughter of Charles and Elizabeth JOHNSON born July 1794, baptized by the Rev. Mr. Oliver, September 6, 1795.

Michael son of Nicodemus and Barbara Gladman CROSS born November 8th 1794, baptized by the Rev. Mr. Oliver, September 29th 1795.

Joshua born July 28th 1793; Zebediah born September 24th 1794:
Children of Grenville and Ruth GARRETT, baptized by the Rev.
Mr. Oliver, September 29th, 1795.

Mary daughter of Edward and Catharine CONSTANTINE born August
25th 1794, baptized by the Rev. Mr. Oliver, September 29th
1795.

Urith Cromwell, aged __, daughter of Samuel OWINGS, Junr., Esq.
and Ruth his wife, baptized by Rev. Mr. Oliver July 31st 1796.

Charles Arthur born March 27th son of Charles and Ann WALKER,
baptized by the Rev. Mr. Oliver, August 26th 1796.

John Howard WEST son of Joseph and Violetta WEST born February
5th and baptized in May by the Rev. Mr. Andrews 1786.

Charles Ridgely son of Samuel OWINGS and Ruth his wife was born
November 14th, baptized by the Rev. Nelson Reed 1802.
James Winchester son of Samuel OWINGS and Ruth his wife was born
September 5th, was baptized by the Rev. John Armstrong 1806.

Jeremiah Yellott and Mary Yellott (twins) son and daughter of the
Rev. Mr. John ARMSTRONG (Rector of St. Thomas's) and Ann his
wife, born June 20th and baptized by the Rev. Mr. Dashiels 1808.

Mary Sterett GIST daughter of Independent GIST and Rachel his
wife born 1st September 1808, baptized by Rev. J. Armstrong,
April 3rd 1809.

Thomas Cradock JOHNSON son of Fayette JOHNSON and Elizabeth his
wife born February 25th 1810, baptized by the Rev. George
Ralph, August 19th 1810.

Thomas born of John DAVIS and Mary his wife June 28th 1794;
Luther born of ditto June 21 1796, Larkin born of ditto August
21st 1798; Emeline born of ditto, September 28th, 1800; David
born of ditto, January 14th 1803; George Washington born of
ditto, August 10th 1805; John born of ditto December 15th 1807;
Aquilla Hughes born of ditto March 29, 1810; William Jameson
born of ditto July 12th 1812.

Ann Susanna JOHNSON born March 18th 1817 daughter of George W.
JOHNSON and Frances his wife and baptized by the Rev. John Allen.

Thomas Cradock WALKER son of Thomas Cradock WALKER and Catherine
his wife was born May 16th 1819.

James William Hickman JOHNSON born May 23rd son of George W.
JOHNSON and Frances his wife 1819.

Kensey Johns, son of Charles WORTHINGTON and Susan his wife born
April 22nd 1814 and baptized September 9th 1818.
Benjamin Johns son of Charles and Susan WORTHINGTON born Septem-
ber 19, 1816 and baptized September 9th 1818.

Eleanora Magruder daughter of Beale and Eleanora OWINGS born June 8th 1815 and baptized September 13th 1818.

William Charles son of John and Catharine BEACH born June 30th 1817, baptized October 24th 1818.

Walter Brice son of John Tolley Hood and Mary Tolley WORTHINGTON born November 3rd 1817 and baptized December 27th 1818.

Sarah Rebecca daughter of Louisa and Charles PASCAULT born March 25th 1818 and baptized _____ 6th, 1819.

Mary Catharine Virginia daughter of Dr. Elisha and Catharine HALL born September 19th 1805 and baptized March 23rd 1819.
Adelaid Josephine Ambler daughter of Dr. Elisha J. and Catharine HALL born September 10th 1809 and baptized March 23rd 1819.
William Henry DeSaussure son of Dr. Elisha J. and Catharine HALL, born 1810 and baptized March 23rd, 18(??).
Elisha John son of Elisha J. and Catharine HALL born August 21, 1815, baptized March 23rd 1819.

Rosetta Usher daughter of Charles and Susan WORTHINGTON born October 29th 1818, and baptized February 7, 1819.

Octavia daughter of Dr. Thomas J. C. and Elizabeth MONROE born February 22, 18(?), and baptized August 12th 1819.

Mary Tolley daughter of John T. H. and Mary Tolley WORTHINGTON born May 7, 18(?), baptized October 31, 1819.

James Inglis son of Philip and Rachel GRIFFIN born March 14, 1815; John son of above, born November 17, 1816; and Edward also son of above Philip & Rachel GRIFFIN was born May 6, 1819, and all baptized November 1st 1819.

Children of Christopher and Susan TODD: Sarah Todd was born 22 May, 1806; Thomas Todd was born 19th January 1809; Maria Ridgley TODD was born 27 June 1811; Susan TODD was born 11 January, 1814; Elizabeth TODD was born 17 August 1816; Eleanor TODD was born 9 January 1819; all baptized by Rev. Charles C. Austin, August 1, 1821; Ann TODD was born 17 October 1821 and baptized by the Rev. Charles Austin January 22, 1822.

Children of William and Nancy OWINGS: Peter Samuel b. 1807; Paul Noldeman and Jacob Brenanian b. 1811; Horace Samuel b. 1813; Henry Holdeman b. 1816; Frederick Augustus b. 1818; Silas Samuel b. 1820; baptized by The Rev. Charles C. Austin, April 7th 1822.

Elizabeth GORSUCH, adult, baptized by the Rev. Mr. Charles C. Austin April 7, 1822.

Children of Levi OWINGS: Jesse born 13 January 1818; Philip Reister born 17 March, 1820; Levi Franklin born 17 April 1822, baptized by Rev. Mr. Austin 13 June 1822.

Abraham VAN BIBBER, son of Washington VAN BIBBER and Lucretia his wife baptized June 26 by the Rev. Mr. Austin at Pipe Creek, was born 21 May 1821.

Eugene Bolton, born April 12; Richard Fresby, born March 6, 1818; Robert Hunter b. May 29, 1821 - Children of James and ____ PIPER, baptized November 3, 1822 by Rev. Mr. Austin.

Samuel Moore born June 28, 1821, son of Samuel E. and Sally SHOEMAKER, baptized September 14, 1823 by Mr. Austin.

Nancy Buckler born October 24, 1822, daughter of Charles C. and Ann H. AUSTIN, baptized by Rt. Rev. Bs. Kemp October 8, 1882.

Brian son of Brian PHILPOT, born 6 March 1823.

John Tolley Worthington, b. February 11, 1820, Richard, born July 16, 1822, Sarah Weems born November 8, 1823 - Children of Nancy and Richard JOHNS.

George Washington, born May 1, 1818; James Wilson, born December 17, 1820; children of Dr. Elisha HALL, baptized by Rev. Mr. Austin, August 22, 1826.

Robert Nehemiah born 14 July 1825, son of Nehemiah & Frances E. E. BADEN baptized by Rev. Mr. Austin October 1825.

Andrew Jackson, born 22 February 1823 and Thomas Beal Duval, born st May 1825; children of Menikin & Margaret JONES, baptized 9 July 1826 by Rev. Mr. Austin.

Henry Sanford born 28 February 1826 son of Charles C. AUSTIN and Ann his wife, baptized by Mr. Austin September 3, 1826.

Mary Ann born July 29, 1824 daughter of William OWINGS and Nancy his wife, baptized by Mr. Austin September 3, 1826.

Mary Isabella born June 26, 1826 daughter of Dr. ____ HITCH and Sarah his wife, baptized February 4, 1827 by Rev. Mr. Austin.

John McHenry born 11 February 1823; Francis born 14th October 1824; Edward Ireland b. 28 August 1826 - children of Horatio and Emily HOLLINGSWORTH, baptized by Rev. Mr. Austin.

Kensey JOHNS born January 6, son of Richard JOHNS, baptized by Rev. Mr. Austin 1825.

Ann Caroline, born 27 February 1823; Edward b. 19 May 1824; Franklin b. 13 August 1826; children of Edward and Eleanor C. GILL, baptized by Rev. Mr. Austin 1826.

Cornelius HOWARD married to Ruth EAGOR (EAGER) January the 24th 1738.

John HURD married to Ruth NORWOOD the 18th June 1739.

Thomas GIST married to Sushannah COCKEY the 2nd day of July 1735.

John HAWKINS married Mary SIMKIN the 13th day of June 1733.

William GIST married Violetta HOWARD 22nd day of October 1737.

John HAMILTON married Sydney BROWN the 7th day of December 1738.

Samuel OWINGS married Urath RANDALL, daughter of Thomas RANDALL and Hanah the 1st day of January 1729.

John GILL married Mary ROGERS the 26th day of February by William Libs, Parson 1730.

Rev. Mr. Thomas CRADOCK married Katharine, daughter of John RISTEAU and Katharine his wife the 31st March 1746.

John CORNELIUS married Elenor LETTLE the 27th of November 1751.

George BRAMWELL and Susanna FORTT were married the 7th March 1750.

Thomas COCKEY and Prudence GILL were married the 15th May 1753.

William RANDALL and Constant COCKEY were married the 15th January 1758.

John PINDELL and Eleanor GILL were married the 6th November 1757.

Thomas HARVEY and Cassandra GOTT were married 16th January 1757.

Edward COCKEY and Eleanor PINDELL were married 19th of June 1753.

Alexander WELLS and Leah OWINGS were married 12th July 1753.

Solomon BOWEN and Temperance ENSOR were married 28th November 1751.

James GARDNER and Jane HISSEY were married 8th January 1761.

Vachel WORTHINGTON and Priscilla BOND were married 17th November 1757.

George RISTEAU and Frances TODD were married 7th August 1757.

Thomas Roades SHOWEL and Phillis Anna BAXTER were married the 29th December 1760.

William ORGAN and Esther MAJORS were married 20th April 1752.

MARRIAGES IN THE PARISH OF ST. THOMAS

Richard GOTT and Ruth BOND were married the 30th April 1758.

Daniel CURTIS and Rachel PEARCE were married 5th November 1758.

John BANKS and Mary KELLEY were married the 18th September 1756.

Robert CROSS and Jemima GOSNELL were married the 13th March 1744.

Patrick CONSTANTINE and Anne BOND were married the 29th September 1760.

William GILL and Ruth CROMWELL were married 27th November 1760.

Amon BUTLER and Elizabeth HAWKINS were married 12th May 1745.

John GILL, Junr. and Sarah GORSUCH were married 20th July 1758.

Benjamin JONES and Honor KELLEY were married 23rd March 1761.

Moses BARNEY and Sarah BOND were married the 5th April 1758.

Thomas FORD, son of John and Elizabeth FORD (FORTT?), was married the 29th November 1764.

Joseph OSBORNE and Urath BOND were married the 25th January 1761.

Joseph MILLER and Mary OURSLER were married 11th September 1759.

Charles Gorsuch, son of John and Eleanor BOND, was married the 1st September 1763.

John PITTS and Susanna BOND were married the 6th February 1766.

Samuel BOND, son of Peter and Charity Clark was married the 9th February 1766.

Joseph GIST and Elizabeth ELDER were married 30th August 1759.

Francis WELLS and Ann TEVIS were married the 20th March 1757.

Nicodemus BOND and Rachel STEVENSON were married 1st January 1765.

James CALHOON and Ann GIST were married 18th of November 1766.

John WELLS and Dinah CROMWELL were married 11th October 1761.

Thomas OWINGS and Ruth LAWRENCE were married 27th November 1760.

Charles ELDER and Ruth HOWARD were married the 14th February 1769.

Owen ELDER and Nancy DORSEY were married 10th of April 1766.

MARRIAGES IN THE PARISH OF ST. THOMAS

Andrew M. CUNE (MC CUNE?) and Sarah GIST were married 28th of May 1772.

Thomas WELLS, Junr. and Mary MAJOR were married 4th of March 1773 by Mr. Allison.

Charles WALKER and Ann CRADOCK, daughter of the Rev. Thomas CRADOCK was married the 1st day of September 1772.

Ramsey MC GEE and Elizabeth GIST were married 26th November 1775.

Robert CRAWFORD and Ann WELLS were married 7th of May 1776.

Peter HOFFMAN, Junr. and Deborah OWINGS married 16th May 1799 by Rev. John Coleman.

William JACKSON and Mary BLAYDON were married 23rd June 1799 by Rev. Mr. Coleman.

William THORN and Sarah SATER were married 16th October by the Rev. Mr. Coleman, 1799.

Richard CROMWELL, Junr. and Mary OWINGS of Baltimore County married February 6th 1800 by the Rev. Mr. Coleman.

Samuel OWINGS, Junr. and Deborah LYNCH were married the 6th day of October 1765.

John CROMWELL and Urath OWINGS were married 6th December 1787.

Samuel OWINGS and Ruth COCKEY were married 22nd March 1791.

Thomas MOALE and Eleanor OWINGS wre married 21st March 1793.

James WINCHESTER and Sarah OWINGS were married 21st March 1793 by Rev. Mr. Oliver.

Peter DELL and Nancy KELLY were married December 1st 1793, both of Baltimore County by Rev. Mr. Oliver.

Joseph BOSWELL and Elizabeth JONES were married 19th December 1793 by Rev. Mr. Oliver.

David GREATHOUSE and Persillah GOODWIN were married by Rev. Mr. Oliver January 21st 1794.

Thomas DEMMITT and Rachel WRIGHT were married by Rev. Mr. Oliver February 17th 1794.

Samuel WRIGHT and Sarah DICKERSON were married by the Rev. Mr. Oliver February 25th 1794.

Isaac OWINGS and Achsah DORSEY were married by the Rev. Mr. Oliver March 18th 1794.

James LAMANE and Mary TAYLOR were married by the Rev. Mr. Oliver 31st ? 1794.

David DICKERSON and Eleanor HICKEY were married by the Rev. Mr. Oliver April 1st 1794.

Robert JARVIS and Rebecca STINCHCOMB were married by the Rev. Mr. Coleman April 20th 1794.

Thomas LINK and Eleanor PRESTON were married by Rev. Mr. Oliver April 27th 1794.

John MOALES and Catharine WEASE were married by Rev. Mr. Oliver June 8th 1794.

Mark PRINGLE and Frances RUSSELL were married by Rev. Mr. Oliver June 12th 1794.

John BAILEY and Rebecca BELL were married by the Rev. Mr. Oliver September 28th 1794.

William JACKSON and Sarah SMITH was married by Rev. Mr. Oliver October 12, 1794.

John Hopkins FOX and Elizabeth JOHNSON were married by the Rev. Mr. Oliver December 21st 1794; by license dated December 20th 1794.

William REILY and Mary FOOSCE were married by the Rev. Mr. Oliver December 28th 1794.

John BARBER and Elizabeth RIDER were married by the Rev. Mr. Oliver February 12th 1795.

Bazaleel WELLS and Rebecca RISTEAU were married bythe Rev. Mr. Oliver May 19th 1795.

William BRADSHAW and Catharine MATHEWS were married by the Rev. Mr. Oliver May 23rd 1795.

Joseph DASHINGS and Eliza MANNINGS were married by the Rev. Mr. Oliver July 14th 1795.

Thomas JOHNSON and Eliza RUSSELL were married by the Rev. Mr. Oliver October 1st 1795.

Thomas Johnson BEATTY and Achsah Chemier HOLLIDAY married by the Rev. Mr. Oliver November 5th 1795.

David LOW and Margaret DEMMITT were married by the Rev. Mr. Oliver January 14th 1796.

Christopher WINKFIELD and Sarah FERGUSON were married by the Rev. Mr. Oliver January 17th 1796.

Thomas MANSFIELD and Elizabeth LAWRANCE were married by the Rev. Mr. Oliver February 24th 1796.

Henry CAINE and Sarah GRIMES were married by the Rev. Mr. Oliver August 16th 1796.

Basil SOLLERS and Susanna OWINGS wre married by the Rev. Mr. Coleman February 6th 1800.

Robert DOWNEY and Rachel SUTHERLAND were married by the Rev. Mr. Coleman 14th October 1800.

William Rose HINES and Elizabeth LAWRANCE wre married by the Rev. Mr. Coleman 16th November 1800.

Job CHAPMAN and Ann SYKES were married by the Rev. Mr. Coleman January 11th 1801.

Robert North MOALE and Frances OWINGS were married by the Rev. Mr. Coleman 2nd July 1801.

Matthew STACY and Jane FLETCHER were married by the Rev. John COLEMAN 5th November 1801.

Joseph SHEETZ and Ruth OWINGS were married by the Rev. Mr. Coleman 26th November 1801.

Thomas GITTINGS and Mary WILMOT were married by the Rev. Mr. Coleman 10th December 1801.

Richard JOHNSON and Eleanor JOHNSON were married by the Rev. Mr. Coleman 9th February 1802.

John YEISER and Eleanor A. HOLLIDAY were married by the Rev. Mr. Coleman 27th May 1802.

Samuel STUMP and Martha B. STONE were married by the Rev. Mr. Coleman 10th June 1802.

Adam SHIPLEY and Ruth CRISMAN were married by the Rev. Mr. Coleman 8th August 1802.

Nicholas Merryman of Elijah & Charlotte WORTHINGTON was married by the Rev. Mr. Coleman 16th December 1802.

Joseph WEST and Violetta HOWARD were married December 9th 1784 by the Rev. Mr. Andrews.

John Talbot RISTEAU and Elizabeth DENNY were married January 25th 1785 by the Rev. Mr. Andrews.

Married by the Rev. John Armstrong, Rector of St. John's Church, Yorktown, Penna. Dr. Thomas C. WALKER to Miss Catharine CRADOCK, at his seat Trentham Baltimore County, February 17th 1818.

MARRIAGES IN THE PARISH OF ST. THOMAS

Thomas B. COCKEY and Mary Ann WORTHINGTON were married April 9th 1816 by the Rev. Mr. Feetg.

George William JOHNSON and Frances WALKER married June 18th 1816 by the Rt. Rev. Bishop James Kemp.

Elias BROWN and Susanna E. BROWN were married September 7th 1819 by Rev. Joseph Jackson.

Joseph THOMPSON and Miriam DUNN were married November 4th 1819.

Edward DORSEY to Eleanor BROWN by Rev. Mr. Austin April 9th 1822.

Edward COCKEY and Urath OWINGS by the Rev. Mr. Austin October 26th 1824.

William F. JOHNSON to Frances CARNAN by the Rev. Mr. Austin February 1, 1825.

Lewis PORTER to Sophia HOOKER April 28, 1825 by the Rev. Mr. Austin.

Eliza CONN to _____ MC GOWAN November 21, 1825 by the Rev. Mr. Austin.

Bale RANDALL died 20th October 1728.
Rebekah RANDALL died the 8th May 1739.

Nathaniel STINCHCOMB died the 29th of June, in the morning, 1746.

Hannah OWINGS died the 2nd day of January 1745 daughter of Samuel
OWINGS and Urath his wife.

Edmund HOWARD died 8th June 1745.
Rachel HOWARD died October 1st 1747.

Richard GIST, son of Thomas GIST died November 23rd 1746.

Elizabeth HAWKINS, daughter of John HAWKINS died 9th March 1738.
Moses HAWKINS, son of the aforesaid John died 24th October 1742.

Elizabeth RICKETTS departed this life the 15th July 1749.

Hanah OWINGS departed this life the 2nd of January 1745,
daughter of Samuel OWINGS and Urath his wife.
Richard OWINGS, son of Samuel OWINGS and Urath his wife departed
this life 28th September 1747.

Sarah GILL, daughter of John GILL and Mary, departed this life
23rd April 1744.

Rachel HOWARD, daughter of Cornelius HOWARD and Ruth his wife,
being the fifth birth, departed this life the 16th day December
1750.

Richard OWINGS, son of Samuel OWINGS and Urath his wife died the
28th September 1747.

Eleanor Pindell, daughter of Richard BOND and Mary his wife died
17th June in the 26th year of her age, 1756.
Mary BOND, wife of Richard BOND died 30th day of December in the
46th year of her age 1761.

Nicholas RANDALL, son of Christopher RANDALL and Katharine his
wife departed this life the 6th day of April 1758.

Peter BOND departed this life the 26th December in the __ year of
his age, 1762.
Richard BOND departed this life the 9th February in the __ year
of his age, 1763.

Evan JONES departed this life the 20th June 1765, abt. 65th year
of his age.

Margret SAVAGE departed this life the 7th day of July 1766.

George HOWARD, son of Cornelius HOWARD and Ruth his wife departed
this life the 10th September 1766.

DEATHS IN THE PARISH OF ST. THOMAS

Joshua HOWARD son of Cornelius HOWARD and Ruth his wife departed this life 13th October 1767.

Francis WELLS, son of Thomas WELLS and Elizabeth his wife departed this life the 13th day of April in the year of our Lord 1769.

Phillip HOWARD, son of Cornelius HOWARD and Ruth his wife departed this life August the 14th 1764.

Susanah WELLS, wife of Joseph WELLS departed this life November 24th 1769.

Anne HOWARD, daughter of Cornelius HOWARD and Ruth his wife departed this life the 30th day of December 1770.

Richard WELLS, son of Thomas WELLS and Elizabeth his wife departed this life the 13th day of June 1771.

Onour ELDER, wife of John ELDER, departed this life the 19th day of June 1771.

Violata GIST, daughter of Joseph GIST and Elizabeth his wife departed this life the 13th day of October 1773.

Cornelius HOWARD departed this life the 14th day of June 1777, in the 71st year of his age.

Thomas OWINGS, son of Thomas OWINGS and Ruth his wife, departed this life 22nd of October 1780.
David OWINGS, son of ditto, died 12th of July 1778.
Harod OWINGS, son of ditto, died 6th of September 1793.

Michael WOLF, buried 21st July 1799, aged about 65 years.

Susanna HUTSON, buried 10th July 1799.

Ruth HOWARD, wife of the above Cornelius HOWARD departed life the 17th November 1796, aged 75 years, 6 months.

Elizabeth STANSBURY, born July 18th 1721, departed this life September 10th 1799.

Catharine ROGERS, aged 86, buried 6th November 1799.

Samuel OWINGS, Senr. died in the year 1775 in the 73rd year of his age.
Urath OWINGS died the 15th December 1792 in the 80th year of her age.
Rachel OWINGS died the 19th October 1782.

John STACEY, buried January 21st 1794. (The Register is of an opinion that there is a mistake in the return, it should have been William STACEY.)

DEATHS IN THE PARISH OF ST. THOMAS

Elizabeth MC GEE, buried February 18th 1794.

Amos JARVIS, buried April 20th 1794.

Edward STEPHENSON, buried June 21st 1794.

Elias DORSEY, buried September 20th 1794.

John CRADOCK, buried October 6th 1794.

Elizabeth SUMMERS, buried October 22nd 1794.

Kersenhapprick MADEWELL, buried 23rd October 1794.

William GIST, buried November 21st 1794.

Anna Maria BEND, buried January 20th 1795.

Nelly, a black woman, buried May 24th 1795.

Sybel West WALKER, buried July 28th 1795.

Catharine CRADOCK, buried August 21st 1795.

Nancy WRIGHT, buried September 20th 1795.

_____ DEMMITT and Joshua JOGRIG, both buried September 29th 1795.

Fredierck CRISTMAN, aged 23 1/2 years, buried 29th June 1800.

John R. HOLLIDAY, Esq. aged 55 years, buried 7th July 1800.

Mr. _____ COLE, aged 55 years, buried July 13th 1800.

James HOWARD, son of Cornelius and Ruth HOWARD, departed this life June 11th, buried the 12th by the Rev. John Armstrong, Rector, 1806.

John Howard WEST, son of Joseph and Violetta WEST, departed this life August 12th, buried the 14th by Mr. Lynch 1791.

Mary Yellott, daughter of the Rev. John ARMSTRONG and Ann his wife, departed this life the 6th of September at York in Pennsylvania 1810.

Caroline Cecilia NEWBY, daughter of Mr. Larkin W. NEWBY and Cecilia his wife, departed this life June 24th of Fayette Ville, No. Carolina, 1811.

Bryan PHILPOT died 11th April and buried by the Rev. Geo. Ralph 1812.

Thomas, son of John DAVIS and Mary his wife, departed this life January 7th 1796.
John, son of ditto, departed July 28th 1813.

James William Hickman JOHNSON, son of George W. JOHNSON and Frances his wife died September 16th 1819.

Mary CROMWELL widow of Stephen CROMWELL daughter of Dr. John and Ann CRADOCK, departed this life March 30th, 1820 in the 43 year of her age.

William CONN buried September 1821.

Dr. Arthur CRADOCK October 7, 1822 (?).

Mr. Richard OWEN, father of Dr. OWEN, February 28, 1822.

Thomas OWINGS, aged 82, September 1822.

Major David HOPKINS, bur. March 8, 1824.

Isaac VAN BIBBIER aged 90, April 23, 1825.

Mrs. Nancy JOHNS, May 18, 1825.

Hickman JOHNSON, October 16, 1825.

The following epitaphs are abstracted from Thomas Scharf's, History of Baltimore City and County, Maryland, p. 864, and Helen W. Ridgeley's Historic Graves of Maryland and the District of Columbia, Genealogical Publishing Company 1967. The dates given on stones do not always agree.

From Scharf:

Thomas CRADOCK (first rector of St. Thomas' parish), who died May 7, 1770, in the 52d year of his age.

Arthur, son of the Rev. Thomas CRADOCK and Catherine, his wife, who died the 23d of February, 1769, in the 22d year of his age.

His brother, Dr. Thomas CRADOCK, who died on the 19th day of October, 1821, in the 70th year of his age.

Catherine CRADOCK, relict of the Rev. Thomas CRADOCK, who departed this life on the 20th of August, 1795, aged 67 years.

John MOALE, of this parish, who departed this life the 10th of May, 1740, aged 44 years.

John MOALE, son of Richard and Elizabeth MOALE, was born in Kinton parish, Devonshire, England, October 30, 1677; emigrated to America in 1719; married Rachel, daughter of Gen. John HAMMOND, of Severn River, April 17, 1723; died May 10, 1740, and was interred in the family burial-ground on Moale's Point, from which his remains were removed to St. Thomas by his descendants.

William STACY, who departed this life the 19th day of January, aged fifty-two years one month and fourteen days.

Thomas B. COCKEY, born October the 2d, 1787; died April 27, 1868
Mary Ann, consort of Thomas B. COCKEY, and daughter of John and Ann WORTHINGTON. Born 25th February 1791; died 31st of December 1859

Mary, consort of Stephen CROMWELL, born 21st February, 1778; died 30th March 1820. Erected to her memory by her son, Joseph W. CROMWELL

Maria NORTH, wife of Eli SIMKINS, and daughter of Robert North CARNAN. Born December 9, 1792; died May 1, 1872.
Eli SIMKINS, who died 15th of May 1817, aged 29 years and 4 months.

Christopher CARNAN, who lived and died an honest man. On the 30th of December, 1769. Aged 39 years.

Rebecca R. TEVIS, wife of Joshua TEVIS, who was born 23d of May, 1794, and died 4th of November 1825

John S. NICHOLS, Capt. U.S. Navy. Born January 22, 1800; died July 18, 1865.

Elizabeth, wife of Henry PENNY, who departed this life October 18, 1795, aged 50 years.

Dr. John CRADOCK, second son of the Rev. Thomas CRADOCK and
Catherine, his wife, who departed this life on the 4th day of
October, 1794, in the 45th year of his age.

Ann, relict of Dr. John CRADOCK, who departed this life on the
22nd day of February, 1809, in the 49th year of her age.
Arthur, son of Dr. John CRADOCK and Ann his wife, who died on the
5th day of October, 1821, in the 39th year of his age.

Erected by the heirs of Randal H. MOALE, at his requret, to the
memory of his father, John MOALE, who departed this life July
5th, Anno Domini 1798, in the 67th year of his age.
Elizabeth MOALE, daughter of John and Rachel MOALE, who died
August ye 21st, 1737, aged 3 years 7 months and 28 days.

John George WALKER. Born July 6th, 1787; died October 18th, 1822
Charles Arthur, A.B., son of Charles and Ann WALKER, who died
October 27th, 1815, in the 20th year of his age. Also, his
sister Elizabeth Hulse WALKER. Born December 10th, 1780; died
January 31st, 1830.
Agnes Anna WALKER, who died March 30th, 1810, aged 27 years.
Also Sibyl West WALKER, who died July 27th, 1795, aged 18 months.
Susanna A. WALKER. Born September 3d, 1775; died May 12th, 1822.
Also, Margaret WALKER, died July 5, 1819, in her 35th year.

George William JOHNSON. Born 17th January, 1794; died 26th
October, 1833.

Francis JOHNSON. Born 22d March, 1792; died 26th April, 1868.

Mrs. Catherine HALL, relict of Dr. Elisha J. HALL, born on the
10th of September, 1774; died on the 28th of January, 1836.
Aged 62 years.

Dr. Elisha J. HALL, born May, 1767. Died March, 1855.

Col. Samuel MOALE, born 4th of January, 1773; died 21st February,
1857. Aged 84 years.

Thomas NORTH, son of Robert and Frances NORTH, who departed this
life on February 27th, 1751 or 1756. Aged eighteen years and
eleven days.

Captain Robert NORTH, of this parish, who departed this life
March the 21st, 1748, in the 51st year of his age.

Frances NORTH, wife of Robert NORTH, who departed this life July
25th, 1745, in the 36th year of her age.

Abstracted from Ridgley, Chapter VI, page 116.
Thomas CRADOCK, died May 7th, 1770, in the 51st year of his age.
Arthur, son of Rev. Thomas CRADOCK and Katherine, his wife, died
22d February 1769, in the 22d year of his age.
Dr. Thomas CRADOCK, brother of Arthur, who died on the 19th of
October 1821, in the 70th year of his age.

John CRADOCK, second son of Thomas CRADOCK and Katherine his wife, who departed this life on the 4th of October 1794, in the 45th year of his age.

Ann, relict of Dr. John CRADOCK, who departed this life the 22d day of February 1809 in the 49th year of her age.

Katherine CRADOCK, relict of the Rev. Thomas CRADOCK who died 20th August, 1795 aged 67 years.

Charles Arthur A.B. son of Charles and Ann WALKER, who departed this life October 27th 1815 in the 20th year of his age.

Dr. Thomas C. WALKER died May 31st, 1860 in the 87 year of his age.

Arthur son of Dr. John CRADOCK and Ann his wife died the ___ day of October 1821 in the 39th year of his age.

John N. RENELL, native of Great Britain born April 1776, died at Baltimore December 5, 1818.

Christopher CARNAN, died December 30th 1769, aged 39 years.

Cecil GIST, daughter of Charles and Prudence CARNAN of London, died July 1st 1770, aged 28.

Joseph WEST, born in Rhode Island, died December 6th 1840, 85 years of age.

Mrs. Violetta WEST, b. 22nd September 1759, died 21st February 1844.

William STACEY died January, 1794.

Sarah, wife of Nelson NORRIS, died June 19th 1814.

Maria North SIMKINS, daughter of Robert North CARNAN, born 1792, died 1872.

Sarah WHITE died September 4th 1807.

Mrs. Elizabeth HULSE, died 1801.

Emily HOLLINGSWORTH, daughter of Mr. Horatio HOLLINGSWORTH, died 1841.

Thomas Henry CARROLL, brother of John and Nicholas CARROLL of the Caves, born 1796 died 1849.

Molly HANCE died 5th December 1820.

Brian PHILPOT of Stamford, Baltimore County, born August 9th 1750; died April 11th 1812.

Elizabeth, wife of Brian PHILPOT born March 4th 1768; died July 26, 1853.

Elizabeth JOHNSON, wife of Samuel, died December 3rd 1805.

Ellin, daughter of Capt. Robert NORTH and wife of John MOALE 2nd, died 1825.

John MOALE 2nd, died July 5th, 1798.
Mr. John MOALE, son of Richard and Elizabeth MOALE of Kenton
  Parish, Devonshire England, born October 30th 1697; husband of
  Rachel daughter of Gen. John HAMMOND of Severn River; died
  March 10th 1740.

Elizabeth, wife of Richard CURZON, daughter of John and Ellin
MOALE died 1822.
Richard, son of John and Ellin MOALE died 1763.
Richard H. MOALE, born in 1802 and died in 1848.

CONTRIBUTORS

Following is a list of persons who contributed toward the building of the church in 1743 as printed in Rev. Ethan Allen's book, The Garrison Church, James Pott & Co., New York, 1898.

Name	TOBACCO LBS	CURRENCY L	CURRENCY S.
Benedict BOURDILLON	2,000		
Joseph CROMWELL		4	
Edward FOTTERALL		3	
Christopher RANDALL	300		
Charles RIDGELY		3	10
Thomas HARRISON		3	
Francis DORSEY		1	
John BAILEY		2	
Stephen WILKINSON	150		
William MURPHY		1	
Dorsey PEDDICOART	150		
William PETTICOART		1	10
William HAMMOND		5	
Peter GOSNELL			10
Thomas GIST			10
Samuel OWINGS		1	
Nathaniel GIST		1	
Mayberry HELM		1	
Thomas WELLS			10
George ASHMAN	300		
Darby LUX		3	
John BAKER			10
John RISTEAU	500		
George OGG	500		
Joshua SEWALL			10
Richard TREADWAY			10
Richard BOND			10
Edward CHOATE			10
John THOMAS			10
Anthony BRAYFORD			10
John SIMKINS			10
Henny SEABOR			10
Peter MAIGERS			10
Hector TRULEY			10
John STINCHCOMB		1	
William LEWIS			10
Peter BOND			10
John SHIPPARD			10
Stephen Hunt OWINGS			10
William BROWN			10
John DERAMPLE			10
Nathaniel STINCHCOMB		1	
Benjamin BOND			10
Joseph MURRAY Jr.		2	10
John HAWKINS		1	
Joshua OWINGS		1	
John BOWEN	100		
Christopher SEWALL			10
Thomas BOND			10
Joseph CORNELIUS			10
Edmund HOWARD			10
Jona. TIPTON			10
William NEWELL		1	
George Bailey GAR			10
Stephen GILL			10
William TIPTON			10
John BELL			10
John THRASHER		1	
Robert CHAPMAN Sr.			5
Nicholas HAILE		4	
Penelope DEYE		1	10
Neale HAILE			5
Thomas COALE Jr.			5
John WOOD	100		
Jona. PLOWMAN			5
William COCKEY			5
Richard WILMOTT			5
Capt. Samuel GRAY		3	
TOTAL	4,400	64	10

49

ST. THOMAS PARRISH
WARDENS & VESTRYMEN

The following list was taken from The Garrison Church, Rev.
Ethan Allen, James Pott & Co., New York, 1898. v= Vestryman;
w=Warden; r=Registrar; d=Delegate to the Diocesan Convention.

John GILL v1745, 1754-56; w1746
Nath'l STINCHCOMB v1745-46
Joshua OWINGS v1756-46, w1747,
    v1752-54, w1766
Cornelius HOWARD w1745, v1751-53,
    1758-60
Nathan BOWEN v1745-47
Thomas NORRIS v1746-48
Wm. HAMILTON v1746
Thomas GIST v1747-49, w1765
John WILMOTT Jr. v1747-49, w1752
Robert GILRESH v1748-50
William GIST w1748, 1752
William KELLY w1749 & 1765
John FORD v1749-51
Benjamin BOND v1749, '51
Stephen GILL w1750, v1753-55
Capt. Nicholas ORRICK v1750-52,
    '57, '66-68
Amon BUTLER w1751
Lovelace GORSUCH w1752
John SPELMERDINE v1754-46
Abel BROWN w1754, v1758-60
Edward COCKEY w1755
William HAMILTON Jr. v1756-58
Stephen Hart OWINGS w1756 & 1774
Jeremiah JOHNSON v1757-59
John STANSBURY w1757
William RANDALL w1758, v1770-72
James KELLEY w1758
Alexander WELLS w1759
Vachel WORTHINGTON w1759
Solomon BOWEN v1760-62
Benjamin WELLS w1760
Charles WELLS w1761, v1772-74
Joseph BOSLEY of Jno.v1762-64
Stephen WILKINSON v1763-65
John DOUGHADAY v1764-67
Francis SOLLERS w1764
John GILL Jr. v1765-67
Joseph GIST r1766-76
Thomas FORD v1767-69
Thomas WORTHINGTON w1767
Joseph CROMWELL Jr. w1768
David BROWN w1769
Gilbert ISRAEL v1769-71
Edward DORSEY w1770

William COCKEY v1745, 1755-56
John HAMILTON v1745-46
George ASHMAN v1745, 1746, 1750
Peter GOSNELL w1745, v1752-54
Christopher RANDALL r1745-47,'51
John BOND v1745-47, 1764-66
John HAWKINS v1746-48, r1748-49
Wm. BEAZEMAN (BEASMAN)w1746 &'68
Henry MORGAN v1747
Richard BOND w1747, v1759-61
Peter BOND v1749-50
John HURD w1748, 1762
William WORTHINGTON v1749
Arthur CHINNEWORTH w1749,v1753-55
    (CHENOWETH)   '59, '60
Samuel OWINGS v1750-52, r1753-57
George OGG w1750, v1755-57
Thomas COCKEY v1751-53
John PINDELL w1751
Thomas WELLS w1752
Robert CHAPMAN w1753
Joshua COCKEY w1754, v1761-63
Thomas Cockey DEYE w1755
Henry STEVENSON v1756-58
William HARVEY v1756-57, w1763
Robert WILMOTT w1756, v1768-70
Samuel WORTHINGTON w1757,v1762-64
Richard WILMOTT v1758-59
George BRAMWELL r1758-64
Geo. RISTEAU w1758, v1763-65
Richard CHENNOWITH v1759-60
John CARTER v1760-62
Thomas HARVEY v1760
Thomas BENNETT v1761-63
John GRIFFIN w1761
Christopher CARNAN w1762
Nathan CROMWELL w1763, v1768-70
Luke CHAPMAN v1764-67
Charles HOWARD w1764
Mordecai HAMMOND v1766-68
Robert TEVES (TEVIS) v1767-69,
    w1779
John COCKEY w1767
Stephen CROMWELL w1769
Thomas OWINGS v1769-71
John ELDER v1770-71
Nicholas DORSEY v1771-73

Christopher RANDALL Jr. v1771-73
Job HUNT w1771
Wm. HAMMOND v1772-74
Walter BOSLEY w1772
Christopher TURNFAUGH
   w. 1773
Charles CARNAN w1774, 1779-1784
Dr. Jno. CRADOCK v1775-89,
   d1784-89
John Eager HOWARD v1775-77
Capt. Benj. NICHOLSON v1776-79,
   1784-85
Robert N. CARNAN v1780-82
Wm. GIST w 1781-82
Edward COCKEY v1782-84
Thomas HARVEY v1784-87, 1792-93
John Tolly WORTHINGTON v1788-89,
   1799-1801, 1818
Samuel OWINGS Jr. v1792-96, 1799-
   1803, d1801
Elias BROWN v1792-93
Wm. STACIA w1793-95, 1799-1800
Wm. DEMITT w1794
Phineas HUNT v1799-1809, d1809
Wm.STONE v1800-05, d1804
Robert CHAPMAN w1800
Brian PHILPOT w1802,v v1806-12
Dr. Jno. CROMWELL w1803, v1806-07
Robert North MOALE v1806-1819,
   treas.1820-22, d1807
Griffith WHITE w1807
Moses BROWN v1808-10
Lloyd FORD w1808
George WINCHESTER d1810
Thomas MOALE v1811-13, 1815-16,
   1818-19, 1821
Jno. George WALKER v1818
Horatio HOLLINGSWORTH w1818, 1821,
   r1822, w1838-41, 1843
John BOND of Jno. v1815-16
Charles WORTHINGTON v1818-19,
   1832, 1834
Thomas H. BELT v1821-23
Stephen W. FALLS v1821
Robert RIDDLE v1822-24
Wm. F. JOHNSON v1822
Elias BROWN v1821-23
Edward A. COCKEY v1822-29
John KELSO Jr. v1824-26
Wm. BROWN v1824-29
Col. James BANKHEAD v1827-29
John TAGART w1828, v1829

Nathan CHAPMAN Jr. w1771
John Cockey OWINGS v1772-74
Edward PARRISH of Jno. w1772
Joshua HURD w1773
Charles DORSEY of Nicholas v1773
Charles WALKER v1774, 1779-1816
Thomas BENNETT v1775-77
Wm. WRIGHT w1775
Joshua JONES w1775, 1784, 1788-
   89, 1792-96, 1799
Dr. Thomas CRADOCK v1776, w1778-
   79, v1780-1816
Thomas BEASMAN v1780
Stephen SHELMERDINE w1781
Thomas WELLS Jr. w1783
James HOWARD v1786-89, r1792-1805
   d 1787-88, 1792-94
Frederick COUNCILMAN v1788-89
John COCKEY v1792-94
John BOND w1793-95, 1799, 1800,
   1801, v1806-13; died 1813
Nathan CHAPMAN v1794
Samuel OWINGS (3d) v1799-1824
Henry CLARK w1799
Richard R. MOORE v1800-05
Samuel C. HUNT w1802
James WINCHESTER v1803-05
----- JOHNSON w1803
Joseph WEST r1806-1813
Thomas OWINGS v1803-05, 1821-22
William JONES w1807
Thomas HOWARD w1808
Christopher TODD v1810-11, 1813-
   16, 1818-19
Walter WORTHINGTON v1812-13, 1815,
   d1813
Geo. W. JACKSON w1818
Thomas B. COCKEY r1818-19, v1819
John JOHNS v1818, 1832,1834,1838
Robert WARD v1816, 1819
David R. GIST v1819, 1821
Col. David HOPKINS v1821-23,
   w1821-23, w1821-22
John HOLLINGSWORTH r1821
James PIPER v1822-26, 1838-39,
   1845, w1844, d1838-39
John PATTERSON v1823-29, 1832,
   w1824-27
Christopher CARNAN v1824-26
Dr. Wm. HITCH v1826-29, d1828
Nicholas C. CARROLL v1827-28,
   1838-40, 1845-48, 1850

51

Owen MAYNARD v1829-1832
James OWINGS v1832, 1834
Wm. TAGART v1832
W. VAN BIBBER v1838-41
Henry STEVENSON v1838-41, 1843-52
   w1851-56, d1840
Dr. Thomas Cradock WALKER v1839-41
P. FORDEN v1839-41
Cardiff TAGART v1841, 1843, 1852,
   w1846
Edward HALL v1843, 1844, 1847,
   w1845-47
Edward D. LYNN v1846-49, '51-65,
   r2848-49, w1863, treas. 1859-
   65, d1859-64
Thomas CRADOCK v1849-96, w1865-
   96, d1869-96
Dr. J. T. COUNCILMAN v1852-68,
   r1853-68, w1852, d1868
Robert RIDDLE v1854; died 1855
James H. MC HENRY 1855-56
Dr. James MAYNARD v1856-61
Alex. RIDDLE v1856-85, w1880-85
Col. ---- HUGER v1860
Dr. John C. VAN WYCK v1861-63
Carroll SPENCE v1862-69
George H. ELDER w1863, v1864-66,
   d1865-66
Charles Lyon ROGERS v1865-77
Dr. Wm. M. WOOD w1867-79,
   v1873, 1875-79
----- MINTTNACHT w1869-73
William Fell JOHNSON r1869-98,
   v1877-98
B. F. VOSS v1878-80
Richard B. POST v1881-88
Samuel M. SHOEMAKER v1884-98
Wm. Checkley SHAW v1889-98
Thomas CRADOCK 1896-98
John MC HENRY 1897-98

Benjamin ARTHUR v1832-34, 1838-50
   w 1845
Rich'd H. OWEN v1834, 1843-58,
   w1838-52, d1844-58, treas.'53-'58
J. HAMMOND v1838
Dr. Edmund B. ADDISON v1838-47,
   r1838-41
J. MAYNADIER v1840-41
J. McHenry HOLLINGSWORTH v1843-46
W. H. MEDCALF v1843, d1843
Franklin METCALF r1843-48
Jno. H. CARROLL v1844-53,r1849-54
Dr. J. C. MORFIT v1848-51
Wm. P. MAULSBY v1848-49
Thomas H. GIBSON v1848-53
Dennis A. SMITH v1850-51, w1850
Lt. J.FLETCHER v1850-52
John ROSS v1853
----- GILES v1853-56
J. Louis SMITH v1854-62
William F. JOHNSON 1855, '59-60,
   w1861
G. B. MULLIGAN v1857-58
Gen.Benj. C. HOWARD w1859,'60,'62
Reuben STUMP v1861-75
R. F. MAYNARD v1862-97, treas.
   1865-97, w1885-97
William DEVRIES w1864
Charles Morton STEWART v1867-98,
   d1897-98
Noah WALKER v1869-73
Samuel M. SHOEMAKER v1870-73,
   1880-84
Charles K. HARRISON v1874-77
John N. CARROLL v1878-83
Samuel H. TAGART v1884-92
C. T. COCKEY v1885-98
George N. MOALE 1892-98, w1897-98
   treas. 1897-98

The involvement of individuals in connection with St. Thomas parish is recorded in the Vestry Proceedings. A chronological abstract follows listing persons involved in activities concerning the parish. A list of vestrymen, wardens and registrars appointed are included in a separate chapter and not listed here.

April 15, 1745: Two books were produced for the parish use, one for the proceedings and the other for the Registering of Births, Marriages and Deaths in the parish. They were bought for the parish by John HAMILTON and Josa. OWINGS.

May 28, 1745: Col. William HAMMOND was appointed "for Levaling the Church floor with Earth, within three bricks of the water table . . ." and on June 8, 1745 it was agreed with Col. HAMMOND to build "a brick Vestry house 16 x 12', within side the walls to be thirteen inches thick above the water table and eight foot high or seven and a half with a good chimney."

July 19, 1745: Same William HAMMOND above agreed "to paint with red the Window Shutters doors windows frames Cornish sides and end twice over . . . "

August 3, 1745: George BAILEY was appointed Sexton.

December 3, 1745: George ASHMAN and John HAMILTON were appointed to purchase "of any person they can, four thousand foot of good pine plank. . . to be delivered at Baltimore Town."

January 21, 1745/6: William CROMWELL agreed to build the "whole set of pews . . . make the communion table, rails and banisters round the Chancel to be made of Walnutt wood . . ."

March 31, 1746: John BOND "is to provide a bason for the church use with all convenient speed . . . "

July 1, 1746: Notice was given that Nathaniel STINCHCOMB had died and a vestryman was to be chosen in his place on the 19th.

August 12, 1746: The Vestry order that "Joseph SOLLARS and Eleanor SOLLARS make their appearance . . . to make their defence for unlawful cohabitation together."

September 23, 1746: Joseph SOLLARS was admonished, but Eleanor did not appear.

April 20, 1747: An order was given to William HAMILTON "on Mr. James RICHARD for one thousands pounds of tobacco at 10 pr Ct."

June 2, 1747: Notice was given that a vestryman would be chosen to take the place of Capt. Henry MORGAN "who being Discharged from the Duty of Vestryman by being Heigh Sheriff of the County."

January 4, 1747/8: John HAMILTON made a "present of a book" for entering the proceedings of the Vestry.

June 13, 1749: Nicholas DORSEY refused to serve as Vestryman by "reason he is not a free holder."

August 8, 1749: A summons was ordered for Charles MOTHERBY and Ann STRANGE to appear to give reasons why they cohabit together "Contrary to Law." On September 5 Charles and Ann appeared only to have their charge postponed and on that day a summons was ordered to be sent to William AMBRACE and Susanah HAGUE "both to appear as Evidences to Declare what they know of such things as they shall be asked Concerning Charles MOTHERBY and Ann STRANGE." Also on September 5 a summons was issued for James RICHARD, a late sheriff, to settle his accounts.

October 3, 1749: The Vestry "Proceeded to Admonish Charles MOTHERBY to put the aforesaid Ann STRANGE away . . . and [ordered] Ann STRANGE to Leave Charles MOTHERBY immediately and not to frequent his company any more as it suspected to be unlawful." William AMBROSS did not appear to testify in the case and was found in contempt of authority.
Also on October 3, a warrant was taken out on William LEWIS, who had a warrant to serve on Domeny Buckler PARTRAGE for the "sum of one pound current money and never paid the Vestry the money nor brought PARTRAGE to justice."

December 5, 1749: Christopher RANDALL was chosen to act as Inspector for the ensuing year at the warehouse in Baltimore Town.

December 6, 1749: Charles MOTHERBY appeared as ordered and "still persists in obistinacy . . . " Ann STRANGE was ordered to appear, but did not.

February 20, 1750: The Charles MOTHERBY - Ann STRANGE case was dropped, "in as much as the said Charles MOTHERBY has put away the said Ann STRANGE before Court."

April 16, 1750: John HAWKINS was appointed to serve as Clerk.

May 1, 1750: Charles MOTHERBY and Ann STRANGE were presented again to the Court for unlawful cohabitating together as were John ROBERTS and Elizabeth BAKER.

September 4, 1750: George ASHMAN and John HAMILTON were chosen for the office of Inspectors for the coming year. Roger BOYCE, sheriff, was summoned to appear to settle accounts.

December 4, 1750: The vestry received a lock of John HAWKINS "which he put to the Vestry house Door" and "came Thomas BOND and begged a longer time for compleating of the Church yard . . ."

May 7, 1751: Christopher RANDALL qualified as clerk for the next year and Samuel OWINGS was ordered to settle a final account with Roger BOYCE.

June 11, 1751: It was "agreed to sell John HUDGE 81 pounds of tobacco at 22s/6 per hd. and gave an order for the sum on Major Thomas SHEREDINE Sher. accordingly." It was noted that Thomas BOND "put good Iron Hinges to every gate and Bolt or bolts to fasten the same sufficiently well, and put a new post-instead of one now broke and to Ram all such such posts that wants it."

September 3, 1751: The Rev. Mr. Thomas CRADOCK was excused for not appearing as he had gone to the funeral of the Rev. Mr. HENDERSON.

December 3, 1751: Tobias STANSBERRY would "Glase the Church windows."

May 5, 1752: Christopher RANDALL was chosen Sexton and included in his duties was to "provide a sufficient Quantity of water every Sunday."

July 7, 1752: John WILLMOTT failed to qualify as a Church Warden and he was fined "as Law Directs."

September 2, 1752: George ASHMAN was chosen as Inspector for the year. Jacob YOUNG was sold tobacco. William GIST agreed to repair the church pews for 7 years.

April 23, 1753: Thomas HUDGELL (HUDGLE) was appointed Sextant.

September 4, 1753: Cornelius HOWARD was "agreed to make and sett in the Church two Benches Eight foot long and two feet Broad with three posts and a Rail in the middle of each Bench . . ."

December 3, 1753: John HAMILTON was appointed as an additional inspector.

May 7, 1754: "Sold to Thomas WELLS eleven Hundred Eighty & Two pounds of Tobacco."

June 11, 1754: Samuel OWINGS was ordered to buy "for Vestry House a good plate stock lock." Sold Adam GOOSE 382 pounds of tobacco, Michael HUFF 520 pounds, John CARTER 900 pounds, Peter GOSNELL 114 pounds, Arthur CHENOWETH 1375 pounds, Joshua OWINGS 150 pounds, Jacob BARHOVER 561 pounds, George BRAMWELL 1500 pounds, Thomas HUDGLE 75 pounds, "all sold at 12/6 per Ct."

July 2, 1754: The benches of Cornelius HOWARD were received. William GIST agreed to "Tarr the Church and Vestry house twice with Tarr and Red paint by the Last of August." An order was given to Samuel OWINGS to call on "William YOUNG, Sher. for the Ballance Due from him."

June 10, 1755: George RISTEAU did not qualify to serve as church warden.

July 1, 1755: The Vestry agreed to send to England for a large Bible and two Common Prayer Books.

June 8, 1756: Mention is made in reference to a recent sale of tobacco to Major FRANKLIN. William BARNEY and Solloman WOODEN were engaged to build a gallery in the church.

July 27, 1756: Agreed to sell Nicholas ROGERS the "Ballance in Tobacco Due to the Vestry . . . in the hands of Mr. Charles CHRISTIE Sheriff . . . and gave Samuel OWINGS a Power to Receive the money due from Mr. Charles CHRISTIE."

October 5, 1756 minutes disclose that William COCKEY is deceased.

July 26, 1757: Tobacco business included an order to to give Nicholas ROGERS an order on Capt. Tobias STANSBURY for "five pounds and four pence and Gave Mr. Sollomon WOODEN, William BARNEY and order . . . and Proceed to sett down the Bachelors in this parish about twenty five years old and worth one hundred pounds . . ."

June 13, 1758: George RISTEAU was excused from serving as Vestryman as being "Overseer of the Highway." William RANDALL was given "orders to buy a genteel Napkin for the use of said parish for the Communion."

August 8, 1758 Peter BOND agreed to "make and put in good repair the Gates posts and pails belonging to the Church yard . . . and to Grub and clear all round the Church yard 12 foot clear of the pails and clear up the same . . ."

May 1, 1759: William GIST agreed to put a new sill to the church door.

July 3, 1759: Alexander WELLS agreed to whitewash the church and "to put up and find scantling timber Nails and other Materials for the same."

July 10, 1759: Moses BARNEY agreed to put "as many new Shingles to the Church as should be wanting."

November 13, 1759: Nicholas ROGERS is mentioned as deceased.

November 27, 1759: Five shillings was paid to William GIST for "putting a new sill to the church door" and it was agreed for Alexander WELLS to make a new window shutter for the vestry house. Money was allowed Thomas HUDGELL for "cleaning . . . the church right well."

December 11, 1759: Alexander WELLS account credited to plaster and whitewash the church.

May 6, 1760: Order Thomas JONES to get eighteen-thousand "good, merchantable Cipress Shingles."

According to law "set down the number of Bachelors of this parish worth one hundred pounds and upwards. Viz. Capt. Thomas Cockey DEYE, worth 300 pounds and Rees BOWEN, Bale OWINGS, Samuel

OWINGS, Jr., Charles HOWARD, John DAUGHADAY, Nathan CROMWELL, Richard RAWLINGS, Richard HOOKER, Thomas HOOKER, Nathaniel STINCHCOMB, Walter BOSLEY, John FISHPAW, William BARNEY, Anthony GOTT, and Abel BROWN, Jr. worth 100 pounds each. " . . . Thomas JONES to hire the Waggoning of the Shingles for the church up to the church yard . . . as soon as they come to hand."

December 2, 1760: Agreed with Capt. Nicholas ORRICK to bring up from Mr. Thomas JONES of Baltimore Town to the church eighteen-thousand shingles and to have them put up safe, and "for said ORRICK to get a lock and key and Staple for the Vestry House door." Mr. Alexander Wells agreed to make a window for the Vestry house.

April 14, 1761: Mr. Thomas HARVEY's account for serving communion for the year was approved. Benjamin BOND refused to serve as warden "as not being a freeholder."

July 14, 1761: The Bachelor accounting was again taken. The list for Bachelors worth over 300 pounds included Capt. Thomas Cockey DEYE, Nathaniel STINCHCOMB, John DAUGHADAY, Bale OWINGS, Samuel OWINGS, Jr., Edward POUTANY, Nathan CROMWELL and worth 100 pounds or more included Rees BOWEN, Richard ROLLINGS, Richard HOOKER, Walter BOSLEY, John FISHPAW, William BARNEY, Jr., Anthony GOTT, Abel BROWN, Jr., Michael HUFF and Aquilla PRICE.

August 10, 1762: Agreed with Thomas REDBORN to "tarr the Church" and agreed with Thomas JONES to buy four barrels of tar.

September 7, 1762: John GRIFFITH's account for serving communion for the year was approved. It was agreed to meet at the Widow ORRICK's in Baltimore Town in order to prove the Vestry's account with the late Mr. Nicholas ROGERS.

April 4, 1763: Alice HUDGELL was chosen sexton in place of her late husband.

June 7, 1763: Mr. Jacob COLLYDY, being "his Lordship's Overseer of the Highway . . . " A summons was issued to Robert CROSS, John RISTON, Christopher SNELL and Amon GREATHOUSE to appear "to answer such complaints as shall be made against them for their keeping irregular Houses and bad Company contrary to Law and also to summons John BUTLER to appear to acquaint the Vestry what he knows concerning their bad & ill Proceedings."

July 12, 1763: Christopher CARNAN's account accepted for serving communion for the past year. "At the same time appear'd the Persons summons last meeting who were discharged with admonitions to them to take care for the future." Samuel WORTHINGTON was excused for his non-attendance as a Vestryman that day, "he being sick."

September 6, 1763: Accepted William LUX's account for Mr. Cradock's Surplice."

April 23, 1764:   Accepted Nathan CROMWELL's account for serving communion the last year.   Charged Henry WORREL for half a barrel of tar from the church.

May 22, 1764: William HARVEY Jr's. account for serving communion accepted.

June 12, 1764:   It was agreed to advertise for the sinking of a well with a well-fixed pump for the use of the parish.

September 4, 1764: A record was made for the wardens to take care of the empty bottles used for wine during communion.   John DAUGHADAY bought the "Tarr Tubbs" in the Vestry house.

August 10, 1765:   John DAUGHADAY agreed to make "Bolts & keys where wanted for the window Shutters of the Church and Vestry-house."

September 3, 1765:   Agreed with Philemon CROMWELL to make three "Horseplat Forms the foundation thereof & Braces White Oak and the form thereof to be fine plank one inch and half thick, four foot wide."

November 2, 1765:   Agreed with Thomas RUTTER "to post & Rail in the Church yard . . . the posts to be yellow Locust four inches by five two foot in the Ground five foot above Ground each and to be well rammed the Rails to be white Oak tenfoot long and three inches by four and seven Rails to a pannell sufficient to keep Hogs & Horses out of the Church yard."

July 1, 1766: Joseph GIST allowed 5 shillings "for Covering the Church Books with Ozenbrigs."

August 9, 1766: Sold Luke CHAPMAN an "Old Bason . . .and the said CHAPMAN to buy a new Bason for the Church."

February 24, 1767:   John PINDELL paid for services done to the church in 1752.

June 2, 1767: Thomas HUTSON employed to buy a jug for Church use and bring water to the Church every Sunday for the use of the parish.

August 4, 1767: "Allowed Joseph GIST nine shillings and nine pence for writing the act of Blasphemy."

May 2, 1769: William GIST appointed to paint the Church doors and windows and "anything that wants repairing."

April 16, 1770: "The clerk to get the table of Marriages printed and a good frame and set it up in the Church and to search for the deed of the Church Land In the Clerk of the County's office."

ST. THOMAS VESTRY PROCEEDINGS

May 1, 1770: Agreed with John FORD to "Ramm the posts of the Church yard well and to fix the Railes that is down . . . and to cut down a dead tree."

July 3, 1770: "The said Vestry reached the bounded tree of the Church's land with the Letters 'ST' as was the mark originally and surveyed the said Land it being part of a track of Land held by the name of the adventure."

October 30, 1770: Entered the death of The Rev. Thomas CRADOCK, which was the seventh day of May 1770.

November 20, 1770: Rev. William EDMISTON qualified as Rector of St. Thomas. Nicholas HAY commanded to attend Vestry for keeping his mill grinding on the Sabbath Day and a "disorderly House."

"Entered Rev'd. William EDMISTON Induction Viz. Maryland . . . Frederick Absolute Lord and proprietory of the Province of Maryland and Avalon Lord Baron of Baltimore . . . Appoint you the said William EDMISTON to be Rector of the Church of St. Thomas in Baltimore County to have Hold and Enjoy the sd. Church together with all the Rights profits and advantages whatsoever appertaining to a minister . . . Witness our Trusty and Well beloved Robert EDEN, Esq. Governor and Commander in Chief in and over our sd. province this ninth Day of May 1770."

April 1, 1771: Thomas OWINGS was paid for mending a church window and he agreed to make one horse block.

April 20, 1772: Job HUNT was paid 2 pounds for providing communion and it was agreed that Joseph GIST would "Rite up the post and Rails of the Church yard that is down."

April 12, 1773: Edward PARRISH reimbursed for "finding bread & wine for the communion."

May 3, 1774: "Mr. Loveless GORSUCH being elected as a Church Warden appeared at the Vestry and refused to take the Oaths to the government." An order was given for Robert LEVES and John ELDER to buy a "prayer Book & Bible for the use of the Chappell in the fork of the falls."

May 16, 1775: John BOND "who is infirm, excused as serving as Warden."

August 22, 1775: Stephen Hart OWINGS "our order . . . for setting up two blocks at the church."

October 3, 1775: "Rev. Mr. EDMISTON has left his parish without Informing Either his vestry or the parishioners."

September 6, 1776: Rezin HAMMOND was fined for refusing to serve as Vestryman.

March 27, 1780: "As Mr. Thomas GIST is unwell and not able to go to the Baltimore Town Vestry, we do agree to empower Mr. Thomas CRADOCK to wait on them in the room of Mr. GIST."

September 18, 1780: John GORDON employed as Sexton.

March 5, 1781: Charles WALKER accepted to call on Dr. LYON for the cash for what wheat may be delivered at his mill.

November 5, 1781: Thomas MATHEWS paid for services as Sexton "two years past."

December 2, 1782: The Church was found "much out of repair, Mr. Thomas GIST and Charles WALKER, to wait on Mr. Samuel OWINGS and agree for making such repairs as this time may appear necessary."

March 3, 1783: The contributions to date for support of the clergyman in grains were found inadequate and the change from payment in grain to specie was agreed upon.

May 3, 1784: Thomas GIST declined to serve as Vestryman; as did William GIST.

June 7, 1784: Samuel HUNT excused serving as Church Warden, being Overseer on the Road.

December 6, 1784: Dr. Thomas CRADOCK and Charles CARNAN were empowered to hire someone to do the church repairs.

May 7, 1787: James HOWARD qualifies as vestryman and is appointed to attend the Convention held at Chestertown on the 4th Tuesday of May.

The tax list of 1763 for Saint Thomas Parish was found in the Harford County Historical records on loan at the Maryland Historical Society. It is a rag-bound manuscript measuring 10x7" x 1" and divided into four sections; Soldiers Delight Hundred, Pipe Creek Hundred, Back River Upper Hundred and Delaware Hundred. Run denotes run, meaning he left before paying his full charges. The names below were taken from the typed copy of the tax list done by Mr. William N. Wilkins of Baltimore in 1959. The names have been alphabetized in each hundred and do not appear in the order in which they were originally recorded.

SOLDIERS DELIGHT HUNDRED

ANSELL, Henry
ASHMAN, George
ASHMAN, George, Jr.
BAILEY, George
BAILEY, William
BAKER, Isajac
BAKER, Joseph
BAKER, Michael
BAKER, Morris
BARBER, Robert
BARDELL, Joseph
BARKER, Ketturah
BARNEY, Moses
BASEMAN, Joseph
BASEMAN, William
BASEY, John
BELT, Benenoni
BLAZZARD, William
BOND, Benjamin
BOND, Samuel
BOOCOCK, John
BOSLEY, Jacob John
BOWERS, Daniel
BOWERS, James
BOWERS, Nicholas
BOYER, Malachy
BRANWELL, George
BROOKS, Humphrey
BROTHERS, Nathaniel
BROTHERS, Thomas (run)
BURK, Darby
BUTLER, Amon
BUTLER, John
CARTER, John
CHAPMAN, John
CHAPMAN, Nathan
CHINOTH, Arthur
CHOATE, Solomon

CHYNOTH, Arthur, Jr.
CLARK, John
CLARKE, Charles
CLARKE, Clara
CLARKE, Henry
COLLYDAY, Jacob
CONNOWAY, Aquilla
COOK, John
CRADDOCK, Rev. Thomas
CROSS, Robert
CROSSWELL, James
CROXALL, John
DAILEY, Toole
DAVIS, Elizabeth
DAVIS, Richard
DAVIS, Robert
DAY, Stephen
DAYER, Henry
DEMMITT, Sophia
DEMMITT, William
DORSEY, Francis
DUNKIN, Patrick
ENGLAND, John
FRIZZELL, Jacob
FRIZZELL, John
FRUSH, Francis
GALLAHOTH, Peter
GALLOHORN, Francis
GARDNER, William
GERVIS, Mead
GEST, Joseph
GEST, Thomas
GEST, William, Sr.
GIBBONS, John
GILREATH, Robert
GIST, John
GLADMAN, Michael, Jr.
GLADMAN, Michael, Sr.

GOINS, Jason
GOODWIN, George
GOOSE, Adam
GOSNELL, Charles
GOSNELL, John
GOSNELL, Mordecai
GOSNELL, Peter, Jr.
GOSNELL, Peter, Sr.
GOSNELL, William
GOSNELL, Yaunal
GOSNELL, Zebediah
GREEN, Joseph
GREEWALT, George
GRIFFITH, Benjamin
GRIFFITH, James
GRIFFITH, John
GRIFFITH, Jonathan
HALL, Elisha
HAMBLETON, John (run)
HAMBLETON, Rachael
HAMBLETON, Sarah
HAMBLETON, William
HAMMOND, Isaac
HAMMOND, Lawrence
HAMMOND, Mordecai
HANES, Michael
HARVEY, William, Jr.
HARVY, Thomas
HARVY, William, Sr.
HARWOOD, James (run)
HAZER, Casper
HODGE, John
HOLDEN, Thomas
HOLDER, Charles
HOWARD, Charles
HOWARD, Charles*
HOWARD, Cornelius
HOWARD, Richard
HURD, John
IGOE, Daniel
IGOE, William
ISGRIGG, William, Sr.
ISRAEL, Gilbert
JACKS, Richard, Jr.
JACKS, Richard, Sr.
JACKS, Thomas
JONES, Evan (dead)
JONES, John
JONES, John
JONES, Nicholas
KELLEY, William
KNIGHT, Benjamin
LANE, Dutton, Jr.
LANE, Dutton, Sr.
LANE, Thomas

LANE, William
LANT, John
LEAVENS, Thomas
LEE, Edward
LETT, Robert
LETT, Samuel
LETT, Zachariah
LEWIS, John
LONGWORTH, Peter
LONS, John
LYONS, William
MANNELL, Samuel
MARSH, William
MASH, John
MASH, Josias
MASH, Richard
MASON, Edward
MATHEWS, George
MCCLANE, William
MCCOILE, Philip
MCLANE, Alexander
MCLANE, John
MOALES, John
MUNK, Reneldo
MURPHEY, William
MURREY, James
MURRICK, Thomas
ODLE, John
ODLE, Walter
ORICK, Nicholas
OWINGS, Henry
OWINGS, Joshua
OWINGS, Joshua, Jr.
OWINGS, Stephen
OWINGS, Thomas
OYSLER, Edward
OYSLER, Ele
PARKER, James
PARMER, Thomas
PARRISH, Edward (son John)
PARRISH, Edward, Sr.
PARRISH, John
PARRISH, Richard, Jr.
PARRISH, Richard, Sr.
PENNY, Henry
PETTICOAT, Nathan
PETTICOAT, William, Jr.
PETTICOAT, William, Sr.
PICKAW, Joseph
PIPER, Henry
PORTER, Richard
PORTER, Thomas, Jr.
PUNBARTON, Henry
PUTNEY, Edward
RANDALL, Christian

RANDALL, Christian, Jr.
RANDALL, John (not in our co.)
RANDALL, Roger
RAWLINGS, Aaron
REASTAU, George
RICHARDS, Isaac
RICHARDS, Richard
ROBINSON, Alsolom
ROBINSON, John, Sr.
ROGERS, Benjamin
ROWLES, David
ROWLES, Jacob
ROWLES, John
RUCAS, Henry
RUTTER, Thomas
RYSTOW, John
SAINT, John
SANDERS, Benjamin
SANDEY, John
SAYSOR, Felix
SEABROOKS, William
SHALMEDINE (SHAMEDINE), John
SIMSON, Samuel
SLYDER, Christian
SOLLERS, Francis
SOLOMON, Robert
SPIKE, Joseph
SPRING, James
STINCHCOMB, John

STINCHCOMB, Nathaniel
STOCKSDALE, John
STODGSDALE, Edward
STODGSDALE, Solomon
STODGSDALE, Thomas, Sr.
SUNKINS, John
TAYLER, Samuel
THOMAS, Edward
TREAKLE, Stephen
TREAKLE, William
TRYAL, George
WALKER, Henry
WASON, Thomas
WATTLING, John
WEAVER, Lodowick
WELLS, Benjamin
WELLS, Charles
WELLS, John
WELLS, Thomas
WETHERINGTON, Thomas
WHITE, Charles (lives AA Co)
WILLSON, John
WILLSON, William
WINTERS, Martin
WORRELL, Henry
WRIGHT, William
YARMAN, Thomas
YARMAN, Thomas
ZIMMERMAN, Matthew

The following persons show as being in arrears account on last year's taxes.

CARTER, Robert (can't find)
COLLERAL, Henry
COX, Samuel
CRESSWELL, Robert
GLADMAN, John
GLOVER, Thomas (run)
HAWKINS, Elizabeth (can't find)
HOLLWELL, Sarah (can't find)
HORN, Ludwick (run)
JORDON, Robert (tho't in Del.)

MCQUERY, William (run)
NASH, John (run-St.John's)
PEER, Malair (can't find)
SEUVILLE, Comfort
SHOAT, Solomon
SMITH, James
SMITH, John (can't find)
STOCKDALE, Samuel (can't find)
WALLEN, John
WILLIAMS, William

PIPE CREEK HUNDRED

ACLAR, Jacob
ACLAR, Volmck
ALKEN, Jacob
BAXTER, Greenbury
BEEKLE, Henry
BELL, John (run)
BELT, John
BELT, Leonard
BELT, Nathan

BELT, Richard
BOOKER, Henry
BORIN, Ezekiel
BROCK, William
BROST, Conrad (in North Hnd.)
BROTHERS, Tobias
BROWN, John
BROWN, William
BROWN, William (of A.A. Co.)

BURNS, Adam
BURNS, John
BURNS, Michael
CARTER, Thomas
CHRISTHOLM, John (A.A. Co.)
COMELY, James
CRADY, John
CREAG, Hugh
CREASE, Philip
CUMMILL, Martin
DEAL, Philip
DEAN, John, Sr.
DEANE, John, Jr.
DECKER, Frederick
DECKER, Ruda
DECKER, Stohl
DRISCAL, David (Balto. Town)
DUNBO, Conrod
EARB, Peter
EPAW, Jacob
ESTUB, John
EVERHART, George
FISHER, George
FISHER, John
FISHER, Michael
GILES, William
GRIMER, Peter
GROSE, Francis
HALL, William (Elkridge)
HAVENER, Michael
HELMS, John
HENDRICK, James
HENNESTOPHEL, Henry
HOKE, Peter
HOOKER, Richard
HOOKER, Samuel
HOOKER, Thomas
HUDSON, Robert
JOHN, James
JOHNSON, Jerimah
KIDDINGER, John
KLINK, William
LAINE, Daniel
LAINE, Samuel, Jr.
LINGFELTY, Daniel
LIPPY, Conrod
LITTLE, John
LOUDERMAN, George
LOUDERSLGLE, Philip
LOVEALL, Ethan
LOVEALL, Henry
LOVEALL, Luthan
LOVEALL, Tebton
LUSBY, Peter

MAGERS, John
MANE, Margaret
MCHARD, John
MCQUANE, Samuel
MCQUEAN, Thomas
MCQUEAN, William
MESAR, Richard
MOLLTON, Ester
MORROW, William
MURRAH, Josephas
NEAROVER, John
OATS, Henry
OATS, Jacob
OSBORN (OSBIRN), Daniel
OSBORN (OSBIRN), John
OSBORN (OSBIRN), Joseph
PARRISH, William, Jr.
PATRICK, Charles
PEACE, Nicholas
PILAR, Conrod
PILER, Ledwick
PLOWMAN, John
PLOWMAN, John, Sr.
PLOWMAN, Jonathan
REASE, Adam
REESE, Henry
REESE, Milken
RICHARDS, Richard
RIDGLEY, Henry (Elkridge)
RINEHEART, Ludwick
RITTER, Ludwick
RIVEL, John
ROBERTS, William
SALBECKER, Henry
SCOTT, Thomas
SENCE, Christopher
SENCE, Peter
SHAKE, Adam
SHEPHERD, Nathan
SHOWER, John
SHUSTER, Francis
SMITH, Henry (can't find)
SMITH, Mary (not in co.)
SNAPP, Peter
STAPLETON, John
STILES, William
STORY, Robert
STORY, Thomas
STROPEL, Zachariah
TRASH, Jacob
UPPERCO, Jacob
VAUGHN, Christian
WELTY, Andrew/Andran
WILLIAMS, Luke

WINCHESTER, William
WOYES, Adam

WRIGHT, Isaac

The following persons show as being in arrears account on last year's taxes.

CAIREY, John
CARBOLT, Thomas (dead)
COLLINGER, Henry
DEAN, Joshua
GORDEN, Robert (Del.?)
HOOPER, Richard (Del.?)
KELLEY, Charles
KELLEY, William
LOWRY, Godfrey (dead)
MAGIS, Peter (run)
MCGEE, Peter (run)
ORGAN, William (run)
PALMER, John (dead)

PARRISH, Robert
RIND, John (in Calvert)
SCOTT, Fred (can't find)
SHRIMPLEN, John (run-Frederick)
TAYLOR, Benjamin (can't find)
TOMES, Christian (Frederick)
TRUSH, Martin (run-dead)
TUMBOLT, Conrod (Frederick)
UTZ, Peter
WAY, John (can't find)
WILLSON, William
WOUT, George

Various items of debit and credit found in the account of Jeremiah JOHNSON, deputy sheriff under A. HALL. Items, not very many, run from the year 1764 to 1771. Among the names shown in these are:

YEAR 1764

BARNEYS, William
BOWERS, Reese
CHILICOATE, Robinson

CORBIN, Edward
DEAN, John
PARRISH, William

YEAR 1765

BAKER, Zebediah
BARNEY, Benjamin
BELT, Jeremiah
BELT, John
BLACK, Moses
BROCK, William
BROST, Conrod
BUCHANAN, Samuel
BUTLER, Edward
COX, Samuel
CROSS, Benjamin
CROSS, Mordecai
CROSS, Solomon
DEMITT (DEMMITT), James
EVANS, John
GALLOHOTH, Peter
GORNET, Richard
GOSNELL, John
GOSNELL, Joseph
GOSNELL, Mordecai
GRUIR (GRUIN), John, Jr.
HEWITT, Edward

KILLYEAR, George
KILLYEAR, Stophal
KITTINGER, John
LANE, Corbin
LARY, Jeremiah
MARSH, William
MORRISON, John
MOTTER, Ester
OWINGS, S., Jr.
OWINGS, Samuel
PATRICK, Charles
PATTERSON, William
PILAR, Conrod
RICHARDS, Isaac
RICHARDS, Richard
SCHARF, William
SHIPLEY, Adam
SHIPLEY, Margarett
SIMMS, James
SMITH, George
SMITH, Nicholas
SNYDER, Martin

STAINES, Thomas
YOUNG, Sull

YOUNG, Vashall

YEAR 1767

GOSNELL, Mordecai
HARRAGE, Elias (?)
MURRY, William
PLOWMAN, John

SILMAN, John
SIMMS, James
TIPTON, John

BACK RIVER UPPER HUNDRED

ABBOTT, Oliver
AMBROSE, William
ANCIL, Henry
ANNICE, John
ASHERTON, Joshua
ASQUITH, Thomas
BAISEY, John
BALTEMORE, John
BANKS, John
BARNEY, William, Jr.
BARRAM, Joseph
BEARD, George Adam
BELLOWS, Elizabeth
BOAN, Edward
BOND, John
BOND, Nichodumus
BOND, Susannah
BOSLEY, John, Sr.
BOSLEY, Joseph, Jr.
BOSLEY, Walter
BOWEN, Benjamin
BOWEN, John
BOWEN, Nathan
BOWEN, Rees
BOWEN, Solomon
BRAMWELL, George
BRITTON, Nicholas
BROWN, Edward
BUCHANAN, Andrew
BUCHANAN, Archibald
BURHAM, John
BURNBY, Thomas
CARNAN, Christopher
CARROLL, Charles
CHAMBERS, James
CHENWORTH, Richard
CLAPTON, Joseph
COCKEY, Edward
COCKEY, John
COCKEY, Joshua
COCKEY, Thomas
COCKEY, William
COLE, Celathael

COLE, Dennis Garrett
COLE, George, Jr.
COLE, Henry
COLE, Samuel
COLE, Thomas, Sr.
COLE, William
COLE, William (Britton Ridge)
COLEGATE, Cassandra
COLEGATE, John
CONSTANCY, Patrick
COX, John
CRAD(D)OCK, Thomas
CROMWELL, John
CROMWELL, Joseph, Jr.
CROMWELL, Nathan
CROSS, Richard
CUMLEY, Joseph
CURTIS, Daniel
DAUGHERTERY, John
DAUGHERTERY, Richard
DEAVER (DEVER), Stephen
DEAVER, Benjamin
DEAVER, Henry
DEER, John
DEYE, Penelope
DEYE, Thomas Cockey
DUMBALD, Frederick
ENSOR, John
FANCUT, William
FERRELL, James
FISHPAW, John
FOGAL, Ludwick
FORD, Benjamin
FORD, John
FORD, Mordecai
FORD, Stephen
FORD, Thomas
FRANCIS, Samuel
FRENCH, Robert
FRYER (TRYAL), George
GILL, John, Jr.
GILL, John, Sr.
GILL, Stephen

GILL, William
GOODEN, Henry
GOODWIN, George
GOODWIN, John
GORE, Michael
GORSUCH, Charles
GORSUCH, Loveless
GORSUCH, William
GOTT, Anthony
GOTT, Richard
GOTT, Samuel
GOVANS, William
GREEN, Henry (Middle River)
GREEN, Thomas
HAIL, George, Jr.
HAIL, George, Sr.
HAILE, Neal
HAIR, John
HALL, James
HALL, Nicholas
HALLOWAY, Thomas
HAMMOND, Benjamin
HAMMOND, James
HARBOTT, William
HAWKINS, John, Jr.
HAWKINS, Joseph
HISOR, Godfrey
HOOKER, Thomas
HOOKS, Jacob
HOOKS, Joseph
HOPKINS, Richard
HOPKINS, Samuel
HOWARD, Benjamin
HOWARD, John (son of Phil)
HOWLAND, John (run)
HUDGELL, Joseph
HURD, James
HUTTSON, Thomas
ISOR, John
ISOR, Samuel
JACKSON, George
JETTER, John (run)
JOHNSON, Richard
JONES, Benjamin
JONES, John
JONES, Thomas
KEEPAUT, Matthias
KELLEY, James, Sr.
KELLEY, Nathan
KING, Henry
KING, William
LANE, John
LEEKINGS, James
LEGREE, Jeremiah
MALES, John (run)

MAPLES, John
MATTHEWS, Oliver
MATTHEWS, Thomas
MILLER, John
MOALS, John
MOTHERBY, Charles
NAILOR, John
NETHERCLIFF, William
OWINGS, Bazil
OWINGS, Beal
OWINGS, Samuel
PARKS, William
PARRISH, Edward son of Wm.
PARRISH, William, Sr.
PASOR, George
PEARCE, William
PHILPOT, Brian
PINDELL, John
POWELL, Benjamin
PRICE, Aquilla
PRICE, John
PRICE, Mordecai
PRICE, Stephen
PRICE, William, Sr.
PRING, James
RANDALL (RANDELL) William
RAVEN, Abraham
RHODES, Showl Thomas
RIDGLEY, Charles, Jr.
RIDGLEY, Charles, Sr.
RISTEAU, George
RISTEAU, Isaac
SAYTER, George
SOLLERS, John
SOWERS, John
SPARKS, David
STANSBURY, John
STANSBURY, Thomas, Jr.
STANSBURY, Thomas, Jr.
  (son of Thomas, Jr.)
STEVENSON, Henry, Jr.
STEVENSON, Henry, Sr.
SWAN, Jams
TALBOT, Edward
TALLEY, William Towson
TAYLOR, John
TAYLOR, Thomas
TEE, John
TIFFIN, Mary
TIPTON, Thomas, Jr.
TIPTON, William
TOWSON, Ezekiel
TOWSON, William
TULLY, Edward
TURNBULL, Frederick

TYE, George
VANSANT, Isaac (Isaiah)
WELLS, Francis
WEST, Jonathan
WHEELER, Moses (run)
WHEELER, Solomon
WHEELER, Wason
WHEELER, William, Jr.
WHOOLF, Michael

WILLMOTT, John
WILLMOTT, Robert
WILLSON, Peter
WING, Valentine
WORTHINGTON, Samuel
WORTHINGTON, Vachel
YAUN, Yowm
YOUNG, Jacob

The following persons shown as being in arrears account on last year's taxes.

CARR, Elizabeth (can't find)
DAVIS, James (can't find)
DEAVER, Ann (can't find)
DEAVER, Samuel (can't find)
DRAKE, Francis (In Pott Upper)
FALCHIN, Phillip (In Pott Upper)
FORD, Benjamin
FORD, Leah (can't find)
FORD, Lloyd (In Patapsco Lower)
FOWLER, John (In Frederick)
GREEN, Joseph
GUDGEON, Mary
HARWOOD, James (run)
HAWEN, Joseph (can't find)
HUDDLESTON, Robert (can't find)
MCCUBBINS, Joshua
MCGUMNEY, David
MUSGROVE, Ant (run)
NICHOLAS, John Williams

PAUS, Nicholas (run)
PINKHAM, Richard (In Pot. Upper)
PRICE, William, Jr. (can't find)
RAWLINGS, Richard
RICHARDS, Abraham (run)
RIGHT, John (run)
ROACH, Samuel (can't find)
SCARF, Joseph
SEALS, William
SHAULD, Joseph
STEVENSON, James
TIPTON, Mary
TIPTON, Thomas
TOWRY, Thomas (run)
WALKER, John
WALLER, Christopher
WEST, Thomas
WHEELER, Benjamin (dead)
WHEY, Richard

DELAWARE HUNDRED

ANDERSON, William
ARNEL, William
ASKRENS, Thomas
BAKER, Abner
BAKER, Absol
BAKER, Bazil
BAKER, Charles
BAKER, Dimion
BAKER, Greensbury
BAKER, John
BAKER, Nathan
BAKER, Silvester
BAKER, Zebediah
BARNES, John
BARNES, Richard
BEATTY (BEATY), Thomas
BENION, Peter
BENNETT, Joseph
BENNETT, Thomas, Jr.
BENNETT, Thomas, Sr.

BLY, Robert
BOREN, William
BORING, Elizabeth
BORING, William (son of Thos.)
BROTHERS, Francis
BROWN, Abel, Jr.
BROWN, Abel, Sr.
BROWN, David
BROWN, George, Jr.
BROWN, Jacob
BROWN, John
BROWN, Mary
BRUNTS, John
BUCHENHAM, Benjamin
BUCHENHAM, John
BURKETT, Israel
CARR, Daniel, Sr.
CHANEY, Benjamin Burgess
CHAPMAN, James
CHAPMAN, Luke

CHAPMAN, Robert
CHAPMAN, Robert, Jr.
CHAPMAN, Robert, Sr.
CILLE, Charles
CILLE, James
CINDLE, William
CLARY, Benjamin
COALS, William
CONDON, David
COOK, John
COOK, Robert
COOK, Thomas
CORVEL, Frederick
CRAGE, John
CRAGE, William
CRISWELL, Richard
DAVIS, Francis
DAVISON, William
DEAVER, Philip
DEHAVEN, Isaac
DIGGS, Exrs
DILLEN, James
DORSEY, Andrew
DORSEY, Charles
DORSEY, Edward
DORSEY, John
DORSEY, Lanslot
DORSEY, Nicholas, Jr.
DORSEY, Nicholas, Sr.
DORSEY, Vachel
DOUGHADAY, James
EDWARDS, John
ESTEPS, John
EVENS, Job
EVENS, John
FOWLER, John
FRANKLIN, Charles
FRANKLIN, Thomas
FRIZZEL, Jason
GARDNER, Christopher
GILLIS, John
GLADMAN, John
GLOVER, John
GOSAGE, Loveless
GOSNELL, Charles
GOSNELL, Joseph
GOSNELL, Peter
GREATHOUSE, Harmon
HAMMOND, Reason
HARRIS, Benjamin
HAWKINS Benjamin
HAWKINS, Abraham
HENRY, Howard
HEWITT, Edward
HOLDEN, John

HOLEBROOK, John
HOOKER, Barney
HOOKER, Richard
HOWARD, Jos.
HUDSON, Mathew
HUET, Edward
JURDEN, Robert
LANE, Corbin
LANE, Samuel, Jr. (Pipe Creek)
LANE, Samuel, Sr.
LINDSEY, Anthony
LOGSTONE, Laurance
LOWRY, James
LYNTHER, Martin
MACKLEFISH, David
MARSH, John
MATTOX, Benjamin
MATTOX, William
MECOLLESTSER, Robert
MESSER, Luke
NEPH, Henry
OGG, Dunken
OGG, George, Jr.
OGG, George, Sr.
OGG, William
OVERY, Brian
OWENS, Richard
PETTICOAT, Nicholas
POOL, Richard
SCARFE, William
SELMON, John
SHAVER, Christian
SHEPARD, Charles
SHIPLEY, Absolom
SHIPLEY, Adam
SHIPLEY, Ezekel
SHIPLEY, Greenbery
SHIPLEY, Margaret
SHIPLEY, Peter
SHIPLEY, Richard
SHIVERS, John
SMITH, George
SMITH, Richard
SNYDER, Martin
STAINES, Thomas
STEVENS, Abraham
STEVENS, James
STEVENS, Thomas
STOCKSDALE, Thomas
STOCKSDALE, Thomas
STOCKSDALE, William
STRAUBLE, Zachariah
STUMP, Peter
SUEL (SEWEL), Christopher
SWOOPE, Benjamin

TAYLOR, Francis	WILLIAMS, Shadrick
TEVIS, Nathaniel	WILSON, William
TEVIS, Peter	WRIGHT, John
TEVIS, Robert	WRIGHT, Joshua
WAGERS, Benjamin	YEO, William
WAGERS, William	YOUNG, Henry
WELLS, Valentine	YOUNG, James
WHIPS, John	YOUNG, Joshua
WHIPS, Susannah	YOUNG, Sewell
WILLIAMS, Mary	YOUNG, Vachel
WILLIAMS, Owen	

Note: The last six leaves of Delaware Hundred are missing. Last page of this Hundred is marked #22.

COCKEY, Stephen 18
  Sushannah 35
  Thomas 12, 13, 14, 18, 20, 35, 40, 50, 66
  Thomas B. 45, 51
  Urath 13
  Urath Owings 40
  William 13, 49, 50, 56, 66
COLE, 43
  Celathael 66
  Dennis Garrett 66
  George, Jr. 66
  Henry 66
  Samuel 66
  Thomas, Sr. 66
  William 66
COLEGATE, Cassandra 66
  John 66
COLEMAN, John 26, 27
  John Rev. 25
  Rev. Mr. 37, 38, 39
COLLERAL, Henry 63
COLLINGER, Henry 65
COLLYDAY, Jacob 61
COLLYDY, Jacob 57
COMELY, James 64
CONDON, David 69
CONN, Eliza 40
  William 44
CONNOWAY, Aquila 61
CONSTANCY, Patrick 66
CONSTANTINE, Anne 17
  Anne Bond 36
  Catharine 32
  Daniel 17
  Edward 32
  Joshua 17
  Mary 32
  Patrick 17, 36
COOK, John 61, 69
  Robert 69
  Thomas 69
CORBIN, Edward 65
CORNELIUS, Eleanor 14, 16
  Elenor 12
  Elenor Lettle 35
  John 12, 14, 16, 35
  Joseph 12, 49
  Joshua 14
  Samuel 16
  William 12
CORVEL, Frederick 69
COX, John 66
  Samuel 63, 65
COUNCILMAN, Frederick 51

COUNCILMAN, J. T. 52
CRADOCK, Ann 12, 24, 37, 44, 46, 47
  Arthur 7, 24, 44, 45, 46, 47
  Catharine 39, 43, 45, 46
  Elizabeth 24
  John 8, 24, 43, 44, 46, 47, 51
  Katharine 8, 10, 12, 24
  Katharine Risteau 35
  Katherine 7, 46, 47
  Mary 24
  Thomas 7, 8, 10, 45, 46, 47, 51, 52, 55, 60, 66
  Thomas Mr. Rev. 35
  Thomas Rev. 12, 37, 61
CRADY, John 64
CRAGE, John 69
  William 69
CRAMPTON, George 30
  John 30
  Mary 30
  Thomas 30
CRAWFORD, Ann Wells 37
  Robert 37
CREAG, Hugh 64
CREASE, Philip 64
CRESSWELL, Robert 63
CRISMAN, Ruth 39
CRISTMAN, Frederick 43
CRISWELL, Richard 69
CROMWELL, Dinah 36
  John 37, 51, 66
  John Cradock 26
  Joseph 49, 50
  Joseph, Jr. 66
  Joseph W. 45
  Mary 26, 45
  Mary Owings 37
  May 44
  Nathan 50, 57, 58, 66
  Philemon 58
  Richard Jr. 37
  Ruth 36
  Stephen 26, 44, 45, 50
  Urath Owings 37
  William 53
CROSS, Ann 6
  Anne 17
  Barbara Gladman 31
  Benjamin 17, 65
  Hannah 17
  Jemima 6
  Jemima Gosnell 36
  Jermima 17
  Michael 31

Heritage Books by Martha and Bill Reamy:

Erie County, New York Obituaries as Found in the Files
of the Buffalo and Erie County Historical Society

Genealogical Abstracts from Biographical and Genealogical
History of the State of Delaware, *Volumes 1 and 2*

History and Roster of Maryland Volunteers, War of 1861–1865: Index

Immigrant Ancestors of Marylanders, as Found in Local Histories

Pioneer Families of Orange County, New York

Records of St. Paul's Parish, [Baltimore, Maryland]
Volumes 1 and 2

St. George's Parish Register [Harford County, Maryland], 1689–1793

St. James Parish Registers, 1787–1815

St. Thomas' Parish Registers, 1732–1850

The Index of Scharf's History of Baltimore City and County *[Maryland]*

Heritage Books by Martha Reamy:

1860 Census Baltimore City: Volume 1, 1st and 2nd Wards
(Fells Point and Canton Waterfront Areas)

Abstracts of Carroll County Newspapers, 1831–1846
Marlene Bates and Martha Reamy

Abstracts of South Central Pennsylvania Newspapers: Volume 2, 1791–1795

Early Church Records of Chester County, Pennsylvania, Volume 2
Martha Reamy and Charlotte Meldrum

Early Families of Otsego County, New York, Volume 1